Donated By

Friends of
Henderson Libraries

An Annual Fundraiser Of

50 THINGS YOU SHOULD KNOW ABOUT THE VIKINGS

Philip Parker

QEB

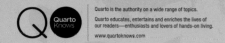

Design and Editorial: Tall Tree Ltd
Consultant: Dr. Shane McLeod

Copyright © QEB Publishing, Inc. 2017

First published in the United States
by QEB Publishing, Inc.
Part of The Quarto Group
6 Orchard
Lake Forest, CA 92630

A CIP record for this book is available from
the Library of Congress.

ISBN 978 1 68297 195 6

Printed in China

Words in **bold** are explained
in the glossary on page 78.

CO T- T

INTRODUCTION

The Vikings were warriors who migrated from their homelands in Scandinavia during the medieval period. They raided large areas of western Europe and Russia, and built settlements there. They even sailed across the Atlantic to North America. Although these raids were violent and spread great fear, the Vikings were not savages. They had a rich culture in art, literature, and law.

THE VIKING AGE

The Viking Age began in CE 793, when the first Viking raiders attacked England. For the next two centuries, waves of raiders from Sweden, Norway, and Denmark terrorized Europe. The raids finally stopped in the mid-11th century CE, when the Vikings' homelands became more stable.

▲ The image on this stone shows a Viking religious sacrifice.

VIKING ART AND LITERATURE

The Vikings made beautiful art from metal and wood. Their jewelry was often carved with ornate images of animals. They had a rich tradition of literature, too. They carved **rune stones** to remember warriors who had died in battle and told sagas, epic tales of Viking heroes, which were later written down.

The day Thursday is named after Thor, the Viking god of thunder and lightning.

RAIDERS AND TRADERS

The Vikings were fierce fighters and superb sailors. Their light, fast ships allowed them to attack towns along Europe's coasts. Yet the Vikings were also traders who travelled far along the river systems of Ukraine and Russia. They were explorers, too, who sailed into the unknown waters of the North Atlantic. They were the first Europeans to reach Iceland, and North America.

▼ *Viking sailing skills were handed down to their descendants, including the Normans, who sailed in ships similar to this one.*

▼ *The Vikings' warlike culture still fascinates people today. These people in Russia are taking part in a reenactment of a Viking battle. Their armor and weapons are replicas of those from Viking times.*

The Viking raids

The Viking raids began suddenly, with a wave of attacks on England, Scotland, Ireland, and France. The first raids were small, with warriors in a couple of boats attacking monasteries and churches along the coasts. These places had no defenses. The raiders stole the precious religious treasures they found there and took them back to Scandinavia. The raiders soon returned with more ships and more fighters.

THE LINDISFARNE RAID

On a summer's day in CE 793, unknown ships approached the small island of Lindisfarne in northeastern England. Armed warriors ran ashore and attacked the island's monastery, killing many of the monks and dragging others away as slaves. They also stole crosses and chalices (religious cups) that were decorated with jewels and precious metals. These were the first Viking raiders, probably from western Norway, and their arrival caused a huge shock. Alcuin, an English churchman at the time, commented, "Never before has such a terror [appeared] in Britain as we have now suffered from a **pagan** race."

▶ The raid on the remote monastery of Lindisfarne is seen as the beginning of the Viking Age.

The Viking raids
The Vikings attack England, Scotland, Ireland, and France from the late 8th century CE onwards (see pages 6–7).

Early Scandinavia
Powerful rulers emerge in the Viking homeland. Vikings seek wealth overseas (see pages 8–9).

Viking ships
From CE 700, Viking ships become more sophisticated, and the Vikings can sail the seas (see pages 10–11).

The first raids
From the 790s CE, the Vikings attack the coasts of England, France, Ireland, and Scotland (see pages 12–13).

WHAT DOES "VIKING" MEAN?

Nobody is quite sure what the word "Viking"means. It may come from a word in Old Norse (the Viking language) meaning "bay" because the Viking ships sailed from coastal bays. Most of the early victims of the Viking raids called them *Dani* ("Danes"), *Normanni* ("Northmen") or simply *pagani* ("pagans"). By the 11th century CE, "Viking" often meant armed pirates. Today, we use the word "Viking" for the whole population of Scandinavia during the period of Viking attacks and settlement. The term **"Norse"** or "Norsemen" ("men from the north") is also used to refer to Vikings and Viking culture.

GREENLAND

ICELAND

SCANDINAVIA

▶ *The Vikings sailed from their Scandinavian homeland to settle across Northern Europe and beyond.*

THE VIKING WORLD

The Vikings came from Scandinavia, the region of northern Europe that is now Denmark, Sweden and Norway. From there, they expanded the Viking world, raiding as far as Spain and Italy in the west and Constantinople (now Istanbul in Turkey) in the east. They settled in much of northern Europe as well as Newfoundland in North America.

BRITAIN

KEY

Viking homeland

Areas settled by the Vikings

| 0 | 300 miles |
| 0 | 500 kilometres |

The Great Army

In CE 865, a Viking force defeats most of the Anglo-Saxon kingdoms in England (see pages 14–15).

The Danelaw

King Alfred defeats Viking Guthrum in CE 879 and sets up Viking-controlled areas in England (see pages 16–17).

Viking weapons

Vikings were known as powerful warriors, who used axes, spears, and knives as weapons (see pages 18–19).

Viking states

Viking settlements include Scotland, Ireland, France, the Netherlands, and eastern Europe (see pages 20–21).

Early Scandinavia

The landscape and geography of Scandinavia shaped Viking history. The people of Denmark sailed between their many islands and traded with neighboring lands. Norway's long coastline had natural harbors for boats. Sweden had a network of waterways and lakes and many skilled sailors. In all three regions, small states began to appear long before the Viking Age.

The Vendel elite were very good horsemen. They were buried with golden stirrups.

▲ *This decorated helmet was buried with a noble horseman of the Vendel Period.*

VENDEL SWEDEN

The Vendel Period of Swedish history lasted from CE 550 to 800. It is named after the burial mounds at Vendel in eastern Sweden. Fine weapons and jewelry found in the graves show that there were wealthy warriors among the Vendel people. Other goods, such as a Buddha figure from Asia, reveal their trade network covered long distances.

EARLY DENMARK

Powerful men ruled Denmark in the 8th century CE. They ordered a huge canal to be dug on the island of Samsø, and a great defensive wall on the main island of Jutland to be strengthened. By CE 808, a king named Godfred had become strong enough to conquer the Abodrites, a neighboring Slavic tribe. He forced all the Abodrite merchants to move to the new Danish trading town at Hedeby.

▶ *Vendel Period burial mounds like this one can still be seen along the roadsides of Ottarshögen, Sweden.*

Origins of the raids

Although Scandinavia was becoming wealthy in the period before the Viking raids, the region had developed separately from the rest of Europe. Historians are still not sure why the Vikings started raiding other lands in the late 8th century CE. Political trouble at home might have played a role, or it may have been the attraction of the wealth to be found in the trading towns of northern Europe.

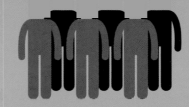

GROWING POPULATIONS

There is evidence that the populations in parts of Scandinavia at the time were growing larger and life was becoming harder. This may have encouraged the younger sons of families to seek their fortunes overseas. At the same time, rulers were fighting to expand their territories. This may have pushed those who lost out to move abroad. Many of these men would have been hardened warriors.

▲ The trade in luxury goods, like this jewelry and metalware, may have provided a powerful lure for the first Viking raiders.

THE ECONOMY OF NORTHERN EUROPE

In the 7th century CE, an *emporia*, a series of rich trading settlements, grew in northern Europe. At places such as Quentovic in northern France or Dorestad in the Netherlands, merchants from Scandinavia traded furs for luxury goods from farther south. They may have spoken about the great wealth to be found at these ports. This may have alerted Viking raiders to the riches they could find overseas.

▼ Rune stones (see page 24) are memorials to dead warriors found in many parts of Scandinavia. They demonstrate the warrior culture of the region.

Viking ships

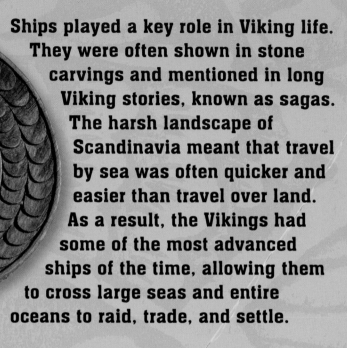

▲ The bow of a Viking boat was often carved with ornate symbols or even the head of a dragon.

Ships played a key role in Viking life. They were often shown in stone carvings and mentioned in long Viking stories, known as sagas. The harsh landscape of Scandinavia meant that travel by sea was often quicker and easier than travel over land. As a result, the Vikings had some of the most advanced ships of the time, allowing them to cross large seas and entire oceans to raid, trade, and settle.

▶ Longships were slim, which helped them to cut through the water quickly.

FROM OAR TO SAIL

Until the 7th century CE, boats in Scandinavia were only powered by men rowing with oars, which meant that they couldn't travel very far. Around CE 700, ships became more sophisticated. The remains of one ship discovered at Kvalsund in Norway had a steering oar (or rudder), which gave the crew greater control. Sometime before CE 800, sails became common, which meant that the crew could use wind power, allowing them to sail longer distances.

NAVIGATION

The Vikings often navigated using their knowledge of local tides, winds, and landmarks. They kept within sight of land whenever possible. They also used the stars when sailing at night and watched for birds in the air—a sign that land was near. They might also have used a marked wooden disc as a type of sundial. This would help the sailors to make a rough calculation of their position when they were far from land.

VIKING SHIP TECHNOLOGY

Viking vessels were clinker-built—they had overlapping planks that made the ship very strong. They were shallow-drafted (they did not go far below the waterline), which meant they could sail through very shallow waters. This allowed Viking raiders to sail up rivers and land on beaches without needing harbours. As a result, they could attack many different targets, making it difficult to predict where they might strike next.

▲ The clinker-built construction of the hull also made the boat watertight.

◄ The ship's wooden mast was made from a single tree trunk.

LONGSHIPS AND KNARR

The main Viking fighting and raiding vessels were longships. Some well-preserved examples of these have been found in the burial mounds of important people. For longer journeys and trading voyages, the Vikings built rounder ships called *knarr*. These did not have so many oars and relied more on sail power. They also needed a smaller crew and had more space for cargo.

▼ A Viking longship could measure up to 100 feet (30 m) long. It was powered by both sails and rows of oarsmen.

The first raids

▲ *An 8th-century religious book cover, coated in gold.*

The Viking attack on Lindisfarne in CE 793 may not have been the first Viking raid. An Old English history called the *Anglo-Saxon Chronicle* records an earlier attack by "Danish men" against Dorset, although historians disagree over whether it was an actual raid.

THE RAIDS RENEWED

After the first attacks against England in the 790s CE, the Viking raids stopped for a while. Then, in CE 840, a ferocious attack on Southampton was followed by others against Kent and Wessex in the south of England. In CE 850, a worrying new event occurred. Instead of returning to Scandinavia after the summer raiding season was over, a Viking fleet spent the winter in England.

THE VIKING TARGETS

Many of the early Viking raids targeted monasteries. These housed rich treasures, such as richly decorated religious books. But the Vikings also targeted trading places such as Quentovic in northern France or Hamwic (Southampton in England), where they could seize merchants' goods. They also attacked towns, sometimes on religious feast days when many people would be gathered there.

▼ *Vikings gather the treasure they have plundered on an English beach, ready to load onto their fleet of ships.*

THE RAIDS ON SCOTLAND

Viking raids on Scotland began soon after those on England. The islands of the Hebrides were raided in CE 794. Then, in CE 795, the Vikings attacked the rich monastery of Iona, off Scotland's southwest coast. Iona suffered further attacks in CE 802 and CE 806. Sixty-eight monks were murdered.

Attacks on Ireland and France

Viking raiders first landed on the coasts of Ireland and France in the 790s CE. Just as in Britain, their first attacks were on holy places—a monastery on the island of Rechru off the north coast of Ireland in CE 795, and the monastery of Saint Philibert at Noirmoutier off France's west coast in CE 799.

THE IRISH RAIDS AND THE LONGPHORTS

The Viking raids against Ireland were helped by the fact that the island was divided into many small, weak kingdoms. In CE 832, the Vikings attacked the rich inland monastery at Armagh three times in a month. From CE 840, they started spending the winters in Ireland, and built fortified ports called **longphorts** as bases. The most important of these was at Dublin, founded in CE 841–842, which became the main Viking settlement in Ireland.

▼ *Rechru Island, today called Rathlin Island, was the Vikings' first stop in Ireland, in CE 795.*

VIKINGS IN FRANCIA

In Francia (roughly France, Belgium, the Netherlands, and parts of Germany), Viking raids were pushed back by the Frankish king Charlemagne and his son Louis the Pious. But Louis' death in CE 840 led to civil war and weakened Francia, and the Vikings returned. They raided Rouen and Nantes and then settled on the Seine and the Loire rivers, and had to be paid off with huge bribes. In CE 845, the Frankish ruler Charles the Bald paid them 5,500 pounds (2,500 kg) of silver to stop them attacking Paris.

▲ *In CE 845, the Vikings sailed up the River Seine and besieged Paris. After raiding and occupying the city, they were paid a huge sum of money to leave.*

As the Vikings entered Paris, they hanged 111 enemy troops in honor of the god Odin.

The Great Army

In CE **865**, a much larger Viking force landed in Britain. Led by two brothers, **Halfdan Ragnarsson** and **Ivar the Boneless**, the invaders became known as the Great Army. Over the next ten years, the Vikings defeated most of the **Anglo-Saxon** kingdoms. They seized land and began to settle in England for the first time.

▶ *Reenactors stage a battle as the Viking Great Army.*

NORTHUMBRIA AND EAST ANGLIA

In CE 866, the Great Army's troops captured York, capital of the kingdom of Northumbria. The next year they killed its kings, Aelle and Osberht. Then, three years later, they conquered East Anglia, and killed its king, Edmund, by using him as a target for archery practice. They also launched an attack on Wessex in CE 870, and in CE 874 installed the Viking ruler Ceolwulf in Mercia, the last surviving Anglo-Saxon kingdom.

▲ *King Aelle of Northumbria views the punishment of Ragnar who is being attacked by snakes.*

RAGNAR'S CURSE

Ivar and Halfdan were the sons of a famous Viking raider named Ragnar Lodbrok. One of the sagas claimed that Ragnar had raided England but had been captured by King Aelle of Northumbria. Ragnar was thrown into a pit of snakes and, as their venom slowly killed him, he composed a poem warning that "the piglets" (his sons) would avenge the fate of "the boar" (their father).

Alfred the Great

▲ *Alfred was king of Wessex from CE 871 to 899. We do not know what he looked like. This illustration dates from Victorian times.*

In CE 875, the Great Army, now led by Guthrum, attacked Wessex again. Its king, Alfred (later known as "the Great"), trapped the Vikings but let Guthrum go when he swore an oath never to return. Guthrum broke his oath and, in CE 878, he attacked Alfred as he was celebrating the Twelfth Night of Christmas. Alfred had not expected an attack in winter and was forced to flee. For a time, it looked as if Wessex might fall to the Vikings.

ALFRED IN EXILE

For months, Alfred hid with a few followers at Athelney in the marshes of Somerset. A number of legends were told about this time. This includes the story that the king was given shelter by a peasant woman in exchange for looking after her stove, but he ended up burning her cakes. Alfred sent messages to his remaining loyal followers to come to a place called Egbert's Stone. In May CE 878, he left the marshes to find a force of about 4,000 loyal men gathered there.

▶ *Aethelred, the brother and predecessor of Alfred, is shown here on a coin. King Aethelred suffered a heavy defeat by the Vikings in CE 871 at the Battle of Reading.*

WESSEX SAVED

Alfred marched toward Chippenham, where Guthrum was camped. The Viking leader tried to attack Alfred at an old Iron Age fort near Edington. However, Alfred's force managed to smash through the Vikings' line of shields and Guthrum fled to Chippenham. Again, Alfred let Guthrum go if he agreed not to return and to be **baptized** as a Christian, with Alfred acting as his godfather. Once more, the Vikings failed to conquer the kingdom of Wessex.

The Danelaw

After Alfred the Great had defeated Guthrum in CE 878, he made a treaty with the Vikings that agreed the boundary between their territories. Over time, the area controlled by the Vikings became known as the **Danelaw**. For 70 years, it had its own traditions and Scandinavian rulers.

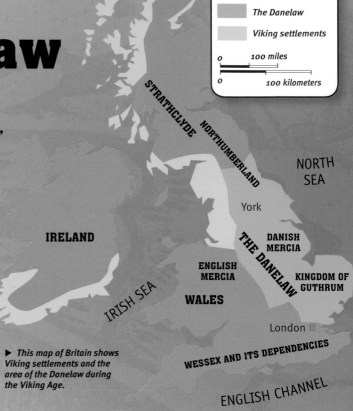

KEY

The Danelaw

Viking settlements

0   100 miles

0   100 kilometers

STRATHCLYDE

NORTHUMBERLAND

NORTH SEA

York

IRELAND

DANISH MERCIA

THE DANELAW

ENGLISH MERCIA

KINGDOM OF GUTHRUM

IRISH SEA

WALES

London

WESSEX AND ITS DEPENDENCIES

ENGLISH CHANNEL

▶ This map of Britain shows Viking settlements and the area of the Danelaw during the Viking Age.

THE VIKING KINGDOMS

The main Viking settlements were in East Anglia, the Five Boroughs (Lincoln, Stamford, Nottingham, Leicester, and Derby), and York (which the Vikings called Jorvik). Viking leaders ruled over a mix of Scandinavian and Anglo-Saxon communities.

▶ Viking leaders in the Danelaw made their own coins.

THE VIKING LEGACY

Place names can often show which areas were the most populated Viking settlements in the Danelaw. A name ending in "-thorpe" (such as Mablethorpe in Lincolnshire) means a secondary settlement in Old Norse, and "-by" (such as Grimsby in Lincolnshire) means a farm. The Vikings also left monuments, including stone "hogback" tombs, with a ridge and curved sides, and richly carved crosses, such as the Gosforth Cross in Cumbria.

The Kingdom of York and the reconquest

The Kingdom of York was the most powerful Viking center in the Danelaw. From the beginning of the 10th century CE, the kings of Wessex began to take lands from the Vikings. However, York remained under Viking control. It became stronger with the arrival of Viking settlers who had been expelled from Ireland in CE 902 (see page 20).

▲ Edward the Elder was King of the Anglo-Saxons from CE 899 until his death in CE 924.

THE RECONQUEST OF THE DANELAW

In CE 909, Edward the Elder, Alfred the Great's son, invaded the Danelaw and won a crushing victory over the Vikings. He built new *burhs* (fortified towns) inside Danish territory and by CE 917 he had also conquered East Anglia. Edward's sister Aethelflaed also helped to take back land from the Danelaw. She helped recapture Derby in CE 917. Edward's son Athelstan carried the reconquest further by occupying York from CE 927–934.

▶ King Athelstan also defeated the Vikings and the Scots at Brunanburh in CE 937.

ERIK BLOODAXE

The last Viking ruler of York was Erik Bloodaxe who ruled from CE 946. His reign was troubled and he was ousted from power twice. Finally, in CE 954, Erik was killed and Eadred, King of Wessex and England, took control. Independent Viking rule in northern England had been put to an end.

▶ Eadred, King of England CE 946–955, finally took York back from Erik Bloodaxe.

In the Icelandic sagas, Erik Bloodaxe was described as a murderous tyrant.

Viking weapons and tactics

The Vikings were skilled warriors who terrified their enemies. They were also fast and mobile and good at spotting their enemy's weaknesses when planning their raids. Viking sagas praised heroes who died bravely in battle. This made young Viking men very eager to fight.

King Olaf Haraldsson of Norway called his sword *Hneitir*, meaning "cutter".

► Vikings fought using swords and axes and defended themselves with round shields.

◄ Viking helmets were cone-shaped and had nose protectors. Some had full-face armor and chain mail to protect the neck.

VIKING WEAPONS AND ARMOR

The Vikings were best known for their axes, which could be used for slashing at opponents. Other common weapons were spears and long knives. The best warriors carried swords, mostly single-edged slashing blades made of strong twisted iron rods welded together. The warriors carried around wooden shields that measured about 3 feet (1 m) across. They also wore helmets without horns and armor made from leather or chain mail.

Some Viking tales talk about **berserkers**. These were warriors who fought in a rage and with superhuman strength. The name may come from the bear skin shirts they wore instead of armor. However, these tales of berserkers were probably made up in order to strike fear into the hearts of the Vikings' enemies.

◄ *This chess piece shows a Viking berserker biting his shield in his rage.*

VIKING TACTICS

The Vikings often fought in small bands that attacked defenseless targets, such as monasteries. However, if they came up against trained warriors the Vikings would form a line called a *skjaldborg* ("shield-fortress"). Their shields acted as a defensive barrier. From behind the shield barrier they could thrust or slash at the enemy. When running forward to attack, the Vikings often joined their shields into a wedge shape to smash through an enemy's **shield wall**.

▶ *Viking reenactors form a defensive wall with their shields.*

Scotland and Ireland

By the 840s CE, the Vikings were firmly established in Ireland, with Dublin as their main base. However, the Dublin Vikings were often attacked by Irish kings and by rival Viking bands. In CE 902, the Dublin Vikings were forced to leave Ireland by the rulers of Brega and Leinster.

▲ This dragon plaque made of whalebone dates to CE 875–950. It was found in Orkney. It may have been used in textile production or as a serving platter for food.

VIKING SCOTLAND

. . . .

Northern Scotland was a short sailing distance from western Norway, so the Vikings settled in this region in the early to mid-9th century CE. There were important Viking settlements in Caithness and Sutherland on the mainland and on the islands of the Hebrides and Shetland. However, the most powerful Viking rulers were the Earls of Orkney, who ruled the islands from the 870s CE.

VIKING ORKNEY

In the late 10th and 11th centuries CE, Viking rulers named Earl Sigurd and Thorfinn the Mighty became very powerful on the island of Orkney. They dominated the neighbouring Scottish mainland and other Viking settlements in the Scottish islands. In 1114, Thorfinn's grandsons, Magnus and Håkon, fought over who should rule Orkney, and Magnus was killed.

▲ Irishmen prepare for the invading Viking fleets, in about CE 841.

VIKING IRELAND

The Vikings returned in force to Ireland in CE 913. Viking bands built new settlements there, including one south of Limerick. The early 10th century CE was a successful time for Viking Ireland. However, after four of Dublin's Viking rulers crossed the Irish Sea to become kings of York, the Irish kings took back some of the Vikings' land.

France and Normandy

After their defeat by Alfred the Great in CE 878, many Vikings left England. For the next 30 years they raided France. They attacked Paris in CE 884 and briefly won control over Brittany in northwest France. In the 10th century CE, Viking ruler Rollo set up a Viking state in Normandy in northern France.

▲ Robert the Magnificent, Duke of Normandy CE 1027–1035 was a direct descendant of the Viking ruler Rollo.

▲ Rollo, the first ruler of Normandy.

VIKING NORMANDY

In CE 911, the Viking leader Rollo made a treaty with the Frankish king Charles the Simple. Rollo was offered land around Rouen if he stopped the Viking raids. Rollo gradually enlarged his territory, which became the Duchy of Normandy. The descendants of Rollo's followers kept in touch with Scandinavia, but slowly lost their Norse language and became known as Normans.

► The Norman Castle of Melfi in Sicily.

THE NORMANS OUTSIDE NORMANDY

Like the first Viking raiders, many ambitious Normans travelled overseas to make their fortunes (including those who went with William the Conqueror to England, see pages 62–63). In the 1050s CE, Norman knights fought in civil wars and set up a Norman state in southern Italy. In CE 1058, Sicily became a Norman kingdom and an important cultural center until 1189.

Duke William, who conquered England in CE 1066, was Rollo's great-great-grandson.

Viking culture

Much of what we know about the Vikings comes from the people they raided, who wrote many bad reports of their attackers. As a result, the Vikings were often seen as bloodthirsty barbarians who had no culture. In fact, the Vikings had a rich culture. They had written law codes, a sophisticated literature, and they created beautiful art.

Local assemblies, known as "things," were often held in open spaces and fields.

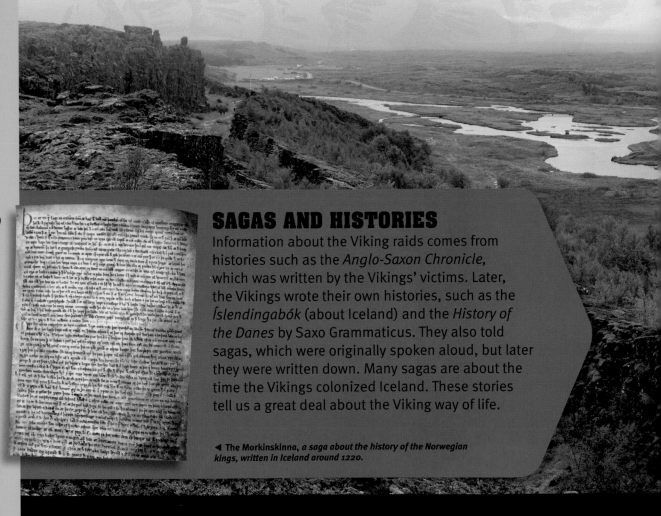

SAGAS AND HISTORIES

Information about the Viking raids comes from histories such as the *Anglo-Saxon Chronicle*, which was written by the Vikings' victims. Later, the Vikings wrote their own histories, such as the *Íslendingabók* (about Iceland) and the *History of the Danes* by Saxo Grammaticus. They also told sagas, which were originally spoken aloud, but later they were written down. Many sagas are about the time the Vikings colonized Iceland. These stories tell us a great deal about the Viking way of life.

◀ The Morkinskinna, *a saga about the history of the Norwegian kings, written in Iceland around 1220.*

Viking culture
The Vikings create literature, law codes, and beautiful artwork (see pages 22–23).

Writing and sagas
The Viking system of writing is called runic. Epic stories are written mainly in Iceland (see pages 24–25).

Viking histories
From the 11th and 12th centuries CE, the Vikings start to produce histories of their own (see page 26).

Viking farms and houses
Most people live on farms or in small villages. The main type of house Is the longhouse (see page 27).

VIKING LAW

Viking society was held together in a number of ways. Many people had a deep sense of honor. They were loyal to local chieftains and to the king. They held local assemblies called **"things"** where important decisions were made and all free men could speak their opinion. As royal power grew, law codes were created. These set down rules and laws for whole regions or countries.

▼ *Thingvellir, a national park in Iceland and the site of the Vikings' first assembly, the Althing in CE 930.*

VIKING ART

The Vikings were master craftsmen. They worked with wood and stone, and with metal to create jewelry. From carved wooden church doors showing Viking folk tales to elaborate brooches and buckles with beast head decorations, various forms of art show this was a culture that loved visual display.

▼ *A carved church door panel in Norway shows the Norse hero Sigurd sucking dragon's blood from his thumb.*

Viking women
Although seen as inferior to men in Viking society, women are often in charge at home (see page 28).

Viking art
The Vikings produce beautiful artwork from wood carvings to richly patterned textiles (see page 29).

Viking religion
The Vikings are pagans and believe in a variety of gods who feature in Norse myths (see pages 30–31).

Viking gods
The gods are divided into two main groups. Odin is the chief of the gods (see pages 32–33).

Runes and writing

The Vikings spoke a Germanic language called **Old Norse**, which people at the time called the "Danish tongue" (*dönsk tunga*). In areas colonized by the Vikings, many Old Norse words are still used today. For example, the English words "egg," "sky," and "read" are all Old Norse words.

VIKING RUNES

The Vikings' system of writing is called **runic**. Its pointed characters were easy to carve on wood and stone. The oldest known runic inscription, found on jewelry from Denmark, dates from the 2nd century CE. **Runes** were used throughout the Viking Age.

LITERACY

As Christianity began to spread across Scandinavia from the 10th century CE, runic fell out of use. It was replaced by the Latin alphabet we use today. Christian religious texts were written on parchment or paper and the Latin alphabet was better suited to this. Rulers and lawmakers were also creating more official documents, all on paper or parchment. However, few people could read or write in Latin. More people were able to understand runes.

◀ *Five characters from the Futhark, the runic alphabet of Old Norse.*

RUNIC INSCRIPTIONS AND RUNE STONES

About 3,000 runic inscriptions have survived throughout the Viking world. Almost two-thirds of them are in Sweden and most of the rest are in Denmark and Norway. Many are on rune stones, which were carved to remember the dead and their achievements.

▲ *The Codex Runicus, a legal manuscript dating from around 1300, is one of the few runic texts written on parchment.*

The Viking sagas

We can learn a lot about Viking society by reading the sagas. These were epic stories that began as entertaining oral tales. They were then written down mainly in Iceland in the 12th and 13th centuries.

TYPES OF SAGA

The largest group of sagas is called the Icelandic family sagas. These tell the stories of the heroic (and sometimes criminal) deeds of the early settlers in Iceland. They often cover several generations of a family and tell us much about the Vikings' way of life. Other sagas tell the stories of Viking rulers, such as Harald Hardrada of Norway, and reveal a lot about the history of the period.

▲ *Grettir Ásmundarson was an Icelandic outlaw whose life was featured in The Saga of Grettir the Strong.*

VIKING POETRY

A great deal of Viking literature is poetry. The largest group of poems is the Eddic poems. These are about myths and legends. We do not know who wrote them. The Skaldic poems, written by named poets, were composed to mark a special occasion or to praise a person. Many Viking poems use "kennings." These replace common words with poetic versions, such as "battle-sweat" to mean blood.

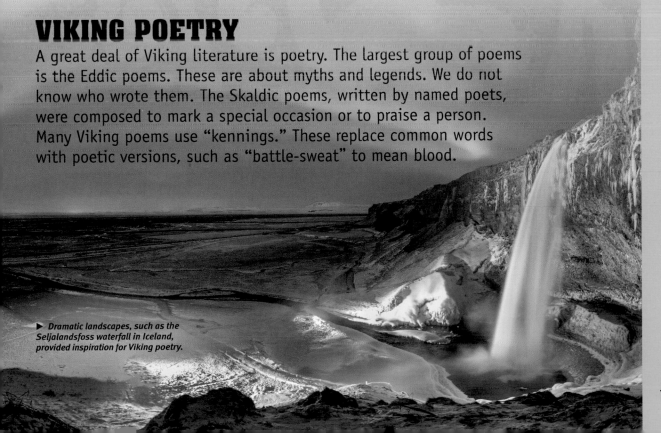

▶ *Dramatic landscapes, such as the Seljalandsfoss waterfall in Iceland, provided inspiration for Viking poetry.*

The word "saga" comes from the Old Norse word *segja*, meaning "to say."

Viking histories

In the early Viking Age, very few Vikings could read and write. This is why the earliest accounts of the Vikings were written by people outside Scandinavia. Only after Christianity took hold from the 11th and 12th centuries CE did the Vikings start to write histories of their own, telling their stories from their own point of view.

VIKING HISTORIANS

The first Viking historians came from Iceland. Saemundur Sigfússon composed a history of the kings of Norway in the 12th century. Ari the Learned wrote *Íslendingabók* around 1130. It gives a detailed description of the early settlers of Iceland. Snorri Sturluson wrote the *Heimskringla*, a history of the Norwegian kings, around 1230, and Saxo Grammaticus wrote his *Gesta Danorum* ("Deeds of the Danes") around 1200.

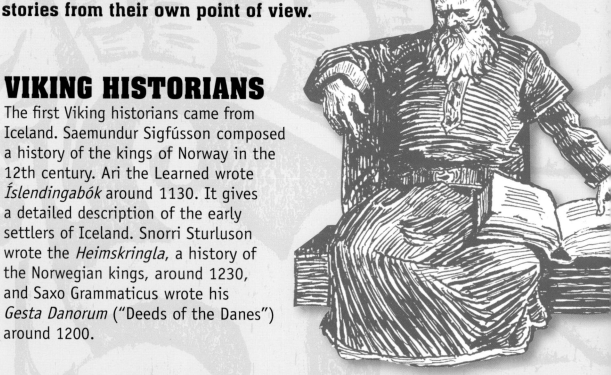

▲ Icelandic historian Snorri Sturluson was also a poet and politician.

▲ Einhard, a Frankish scholar (CE 775–840), describes the Viking raids in his biography of the Frankish ruler Charlemagne.

OTHER ACCOUNTS OF THE VIKINGS

Histories written by the Vikings' victims do perhaps exaggerate the Vikings' violence. However, they also contain very important information about the dates and locations of the Viking raids. The *Anglo-Saxon Chronicle* was created in the late 9th century CE. It describes the Viking attacks in England, especially those against the kingdom of Wessex, where the chronicle was written.

Viking farm- and houses

Viking society was mainly rural. There were very few towns. Most people lived on isolated farms or in small villages. The Viking economy depended on agriculture, fishing, and hunting. Many people only just managed to feed themselves, so any additional income from raids overseas was welcomed.

VIKING HOUSES

The main type of house was the **longhouse**, which was built of timber. A fire provided warmth for the families living inside. Sometimes animals were housed at one end of the building. There was not much furniture—just a chest for valuable items, and some wooden benches arranged around the wall.

▼ *This reconstructed longhouse is in the Lofoten Islands, Norway.*

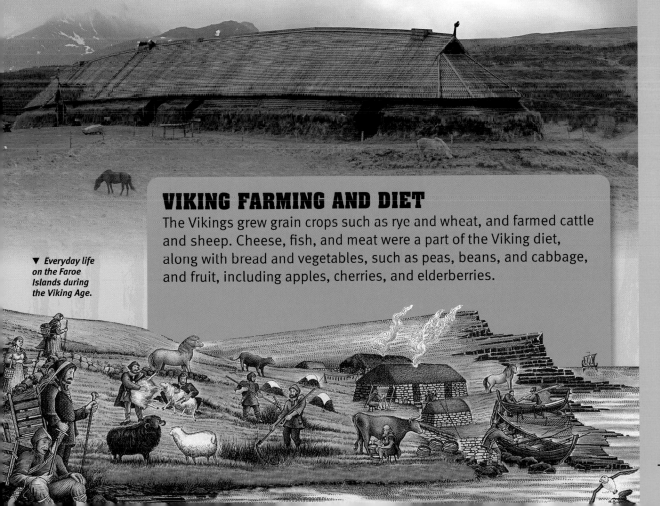

▼ *Everyday life on the Faroe Islands during the Viking Age.*

VIKING FARMING AND DIET

The Vikings grew grain crops such as rye and wheat, and farmed cattle and sheep. Cheese, fish, and meat were a part of the Viking diet, along with bread and vegetables, such as peas, beans, and cabbage, and fruit, including apples, cherries, and elderberries.

The Vikings drank from wooden cups or drinking horns, made from cow or goat horns.

Viking women

Women held an inferior position to men in Viking society, but they were still highly respected. Women were in charge of the home. As a symbol of their authority, they kept the keys to the family treasure chest on their belts. Some Viking women were involved in trade. However, women could not take legal actions in court or hold a noble title of their own, and few girls received an education.

PEACE MAKERS

In wealthy families, women played an important role as "peace weavers." This meant that when they married they made peace between one family and another. Many noblewomen, such as Aud the Deep-Minded, were major characters in the sagas. Aud led a large group of settlers to Iceland around CE 900. Royal women were greatly respected. In the Oseberg ship-burial in Norway two noblewomen were buried with magnificent wooden sleighs and buckets.

◀ This Viking key from around CE 900 would have hung from a wife's belt.

◀ Viking women often wore linen headscarves over their hair.

WOMEN'S CLOTHES

Viking women wore an ankle-length shift. Over this they placed a pinafore dress with shoulder straps that were held in place by a pair of oval brooches. They wore necklaces with strings of glass and semi-precious stones and sometimes a cloak fastened with another brooch. Around their waist they wore a belt, often with a knife, purse, and the household's keys attached.

Viking art

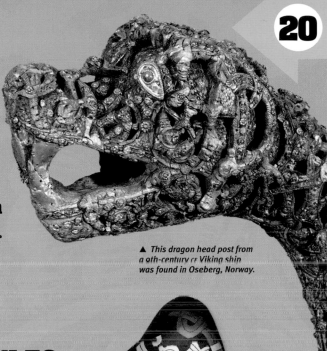

The Vikings were skilled craftsmen. Materials such as wood, bone, and antler were carved with images of animals and plants. Textiles were woven and dyed with detailed patterns. Beautiful objects, such as jewelry, featured repeating patterns of fantastic beasts.

▲ This dragon head post from a 9th-century CE Viking ship was found in Oseberg, Norway.

VIKING ARTISTIC STYLES

Viking art went through a series of styles. The Oseberg style, which was fashionable around CE 800, had animals gripping onto other animals. The Borre style had complex knot patterns. The Jellinge style, popular from the 10th century CE, featured animals and patterns of leaves.

▶ This is a colored replica of a famous rune stone in Denmark called the Jelling Stone. It features a giant snake attacking a lion.

VIKING JEWELRY

Viking women wore long necklaces of colored beads and semi-precious stones such as amber. The brooches they used to fasten their clothes were also highly decorated. Viking men wore beautiful neck rings of iron, silver, and gold, with the ends often carved into the shape of animal heads. Belt buckles and animal harnesses were also decorated with animal symbols.

▼ This gold Viking jewelry was found on the German island of Hiddensee in the Baltic Sea. It dates from the 10th century CE.

The animals featured in Viking art include snakes, wolves, birds, and fanciful beasts.

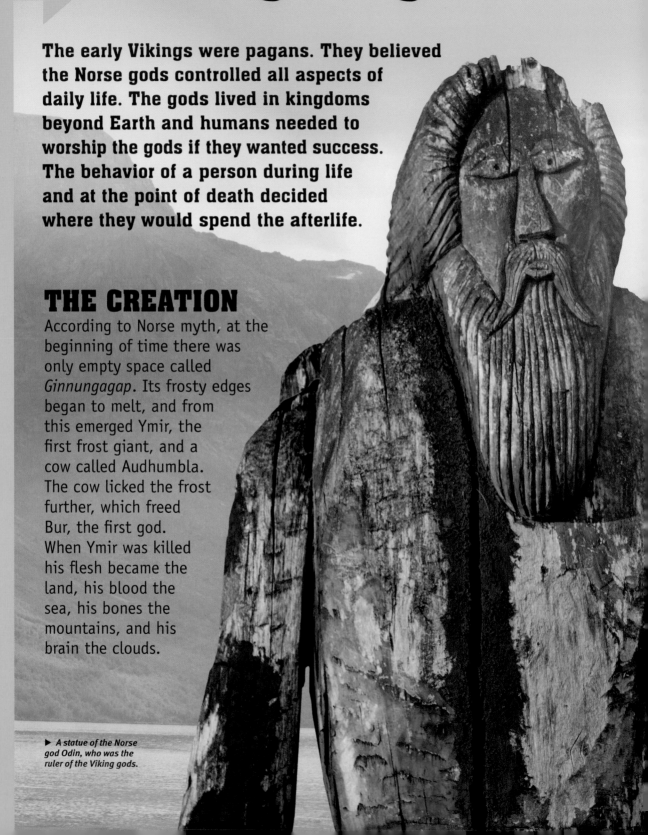

Viking religion

The early Vikings were pagans. They believed the Norse gods controlled all aspects of daily life. The gods lived in kingdoms beyond Earth and humans needed to worship the gods if they wanted success. The behavior of a person during life and at the point of death decided where they would spend the afterlife.

THE CREATION

According to Norse myth, at the beginning of time there was only empty space called *Ginnungagap*. Its frosty edges began to melt, and from this emerged Ymir, the first frost giant, and a cow called Audhumbla. The cow licked the frost further, which freed Bur, the first god. When Ymir was killed his flesh became the land, his blood the sea, his bones the mountains, and his brain the clouds.

▶ A statue of the Norse god Odin, who was the ruler of the Viking gods.

The gods had their own personalities. For example, Thor was strong but not very smart.

30

In Viking belief, the central realm of the world was **Midgard**, where humans lived. Above this was **Asgard**, home to the gods and the gods' feasting halls and palaces. Beneath Midgard was **Utgard** ("the outer place") where the giants and other evil beings lived. **Yggdrasil**, a gigantic ash tree, held the three realms together. At its foot lived the mysterious Norns, three women who spun the threads that decided the fate of all men.

◄ *The first level was Asgard, the home of the gods.*

► *Bifrost, also known as the Rainbow Bridge, connected Asgard and Midgard.*

▼ *Midgard, or "Middle Earth," was the realm of humans.*

► *Below this lay the hellish Utgard.*

THE HOMES OF THE GODS

Vikings believed that the gods lived in great halls, where they feasted with the dead who had been chosen as their followers. Odin's hall, **Valhalla**, was the most famous hall. Viking warriors who had died bravely in battle were carried up by **Valkyries** (female warrior spirits) to spend their afterlife at Valhalla. Those who died in their beds or of disease were sent to **Elvidner**, the hall of Hel, a place of cold, damp, hunger, and misery.

► *Hilde was one of the Valkyries. She found heroes who had been killed on the battlefield and carried them up to Odin's hall, Valhalla.*

Viking gods and stories

There were two groups of Viking gods. The **Aesir** group included Odin, the ruler of the gods, and Thor, the thunder god. The **Vanir** group included Freyr, god of prosperity and fine weather, and his sister Freyja, goddess of love and war. The Vikings also believed in other magical beings, such as giants and dwarves.

◄ *In a dramatic scene from Richard Wagner's opera* Das Rheingold, *the goddess Freyja is seized by the giants Fafnir and Fasolt.*

Surt

THE MAIN GODS

⚜ Odin was the most important of the gods and known as the "All-Father." His two ravens Huginn and Muninn circled the world each day to report back on events in Midgard (see page 31).

⚜ Thor, the thunder god, was more widely worshipped by the Vikings than Odin. He caused lightning when he threw his great hammer, Mjölnir.

⚜ Loki, the trickster god, was the son of a giantess. He often played tricks on the other gods and sided with the giants.

SOURCES FOR THE VIKING MYTHS

The Vikings worshiped their gods at temples and shrines, but almost none of these have survived. Some descriptions of them come from Christian sources. Adam of Bremen's account from CE 1073 tells of a cult center in Sweden where many sacrifices of animals were made every ninth year. The Eddic poems, collected in the 13th century, also give us an insight into Viking worship.

▲ *This copy of a 9th-century CE cult statue of Thor (holding his hammer) was found in Iceland.*

RAGNARÖK

The Vikings thought the world would end in Ragnarök, a huge battle between the gods and the evil creatures of Utgard. The monstrous wolf Fenrir would swallow the Sun and the serpent Jörmungand would attack Midgard. Thor would kill Jörmungand but he would be killed as the dying snake spat venom at him. Fenrir would kill Odin and then the sword of the fire-giant Surt would set light to the world and burn it to ashes. In the end, several young gods would survive and begin the world again, but this time without the threat of the giants and other evil beings.

▼ *A 19th-century engraving shows Ragnarök, the immense battle between the Viking gods and evil creatures.*

Odin

Fenrir

Thor

Jörmungand

23

The Viking expansion

The Vikings' ships were not just for raiding. They were also used to search for new trading routes and places to settle. From the 10th century CE, the Vikings sailed across the Atlantic as far as Greenland and North America. Swedish Vikings sailed down the rivers of Russia and Ukraine and started settlements there.

THE DISCOVERY OF ICELAND

Viking sagas tell of several voyagers who came across the uninhabited island of Iceland, probably in the mid-9th century CE. Around CE 874, Ingólfur Arnarson and Hjorleifur Hródmarsson led an expedition that settled and divided up the island (a process known as *landnám* or "land taking"). They founded a Viking colony that remained independent of the Norwegian kings for almost four centuries.

▶ *Ingólfur Arnarson and others establish the settlement of Reykjavik in Iceland.*

The Viking expansion
From the 10th century CE, Vikings sail west across the Atlantic and east as far as Russia (see pages 34–35).

The Faroes
The Vikings reach the Faroes around CE 825 and build a settlement on the islands (see pages 36–37).

Iceland
Viking ships land in Iceland in CE 874 and divide the land among the early settlers (see pages 36–37).

The Althing
Viking Icelanders set up an assembly called the Althing, held each summer from CE 930 (see page 37).

THE DISCOVERY OF GREENLAND

There had long been rumors among Icelandic Vikings of a land farther west. Around CE 980, Erik the Red, exiled from Iceland as punishment for murder, set out in search of it. He sailed along the frozen coastline of Greenland until he found more sheltered fjords along the coast. Here, the Vikings built a series of settlements and farms that survived until the 15th century.

▲ An artist's impression shows the Greenland Vikings braving the icy waters of the North Atlantic during their crossing to Newfoundland.

VINLAND

Around CE 1000, Vikings from Greenland stumbled upon land even farther west, on the coast of North America. They called it Vinland and established a colony there, although conflict with Native Americans forced them to leave. All trace of Vinland was lost, and many doubted it had existed until archaeologists from Norway found the remains of a Viking settlement in Newfoundland in 1961.

▲ Erik the Red called the icy land he discovered "Greenland," hoping that the name would attract settlers.

VIKINGS IN THE EAST

Scandinavians had settled on the southern shores of the Baltic Sea around CE 650. A hundred years later they had pushed as far as modern St. Petersburg in Russia. Viking fur traders built settlements such as Novgorod and Kiev. These Scandinavian incomers mixed with the local Slavic peoples. Their settlements developed into the states of medieval Russia.

Greenland
Boats of Viking settlers, led by Erik the Red, arrive in Greenland in CE 986 (see pages 38–39).

Viking America
A land the Vikings call Vinland in North America is settled briefly around CE 1000 (see pages 40–41).

End of the colonies
The Viking settlements on Greenland disappear by the 15th century (see pages 42–43).

Russia and the east
Swedish Viking traders sail down rivers in Russia in CE 750 and build settlements (see pages 44–45).

The Faroes and Iceland

One of the Vikings' first expeditions into the Atlantic was to the Faroes. These are a cluster of 18 islands that lie 350 miles (550 km) west of Norway. The Vikings arrived around CE 825 and built settlements at Kvívík and Toftanes. The Faroes became a stepping stone to Iceland, but they did not hold much political power in the Viking world.

THE FOUNDATION OF ICELAND

There were stories about Irish monks discovering Iceland before the Vikings, but the island was uninhabited when the first settlers arrived around CE 874. The later *Landnámabók* ("Book of the Settlement") described how these earliest settlers, who were from Norway, divided up the land in the fertile strip along the coasts. By CE 930, all the land had been settled.

▼ *The parliament house of Iceland, the Althing, moved to the capital city of Reykjavik in 1845.*

Iceland's national assembly, the Althing, was originally held outdoors every summer.

▶ A view over the Funningsfjørður fjord in the Faroes on a bleak October evening. In the distance is the island of Kalsoy.

▶ The ruins of a Viking farm were found in Stöng in the Thjorsardalur Valley, Iceland. This is a reconstruction of the excavated ruins at Stöng.

ICELANDIC SOCIETY

Vikings in Iceland were farmers, especially of sheep and cattle. They remained independent of Norway. Icelandic society was headed by **goðar** (chieftains). They were powerful because people pledged their allegiance to them. In CE 930, the Icelanders established a national assembly, the Althing. The 48 *goðar* representatives were guided by an elected Lawspeaker. The Althing made new laws and judged legal disagreements between people.

▶ The Lawspeaker, who sat on the Law Rock, was at the center of the Althing outdoor assembly.

Viking Greenland

▲ *A reconstruction of Erik the Red's farmhouse at Brattahlid, Greenland.*

When Erik the Red returned to Iceland in CE 985 after a three-year exile, he brought news of a place he called "Greenland." A year later, 25 boats full of colonists were sailing the 500 kilometres west from Iceland. They settled on the west coast of Greenland, and Erik's farm at Brattahlid became the center of a new Viking colony.

EASTERN AND WESTERN SETTLEMENT

The settlers found that most of Greenland's coast was completely covered with ice. However, to the west there was just enough sheltered land in fjords to start two communities, the Eastern and Western Settlements. Life there was harsh, and the population of Viking Greenland never exceeded 5,000 people. People on ships that had landed on the eastern coast perished. Four years after a shipwreck there in 1125, a sole survivor was found who had been driven mad by the isolation and cold.

LIFE IN GREENLAND

The Greenland Vikings farmed sheep and cattle, as it was too cold to grow many crops. They did not fish much or learn to harpoon, but they did hunt the seals that came close to the shore. They also made hunting expeditions to northern Greenland, which they called Norðsetur, but this was mainly for walruses, whose tusks were made of valuable ivory. No trees grew on Greenland. For timber, the Greenlanders depended on trade with Iceland and Norway. The colonies did not thrive. Had the Viking settlers tried to fish, rather than farm, they might have had more success. Instead, as time went by, fewer and fewer ships visited.

▲ These ruins are all that remain of Garðar, once the religious center of Greenland's Eastern Settlement after the conversion of Christianity.

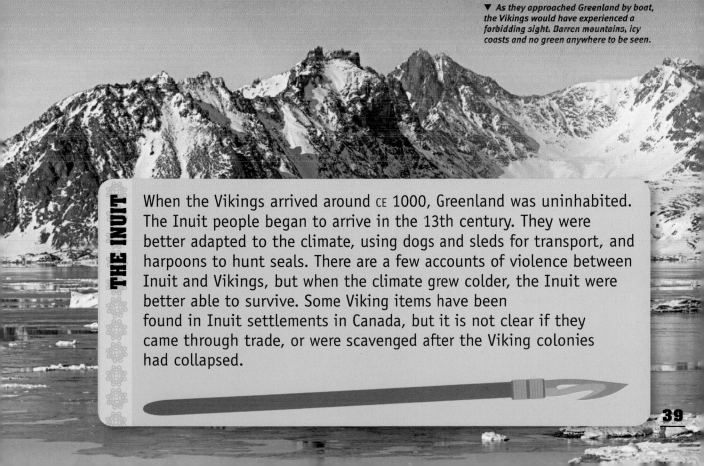

▼ As they approached Greenland by boat, the Vikings would have experienced a forbidding sight. Barren mountains, icy coasts and no green anywhere to be seen.

THE INUIT

When the Vikings arrived around CE 1000, Greenland was uninhabited. The Inuit people began to arrive in the 13th century. They were better adapted to the climate, using dogs and sleds for transport, and harpoons to hunt seals. There are a few accounts of violence between Inuit and Vikings, but when the climate grew colder, the Inuit were better able to survive. Some Viking items have been found in Inuit settlements in Canada, but it is not clear if they came through trade, or were scavenged after the Viking colonies had collapsed.

Viking America

The Viking sagas disagree about who discovered land west of Greenland around CE 1000. One saga claimed that it was Bjarni Herjólfsson, another that it was Leif Eriksson, the son of Erik the Red, founder of Viking Greenland. Further voyages followed, but attempts to settle in North America were abandoned after attacks by Native Americans.

VIOLENT CLASHES

According to the sagas, the Vikings found a rocky land (Helluland), a wooded land (Markland), and then Vinland, where they built "booths" (small settlements to provide shelter during voyages). They then came across Native Americans whom they called *skraelings* ("wretches"). After some attempts to trade with them, violent clashes followed. In the end, the Vikings abandoned the settlement and returned to Greenland.

One saga says Erik the Red's daughter Freydis was one of the last Vikings in America.

FINDING VINLAND

In 1961, the Norwegian archaeologists Helge Instad and Anne Stine Ingstad excavated mounds at L'Anse aux Meadows in Newfoundland, Canada. This was the first evidence of the Vinland settlement as described in the Viking sagas. The remains of two Viking longhouses and an iron forge were discovered. These proved that the stories of Viking voyages to North America were true.

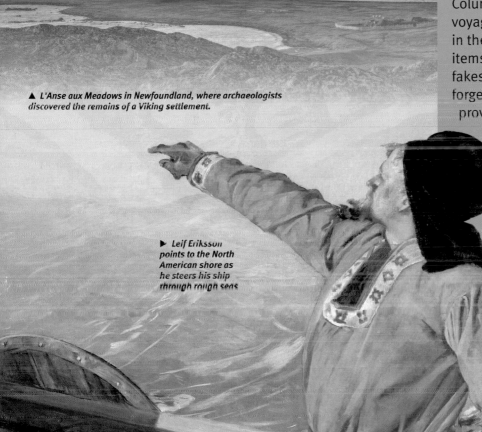

▲ L'Anse aux Meadows in Newfoundland, where archaeologists discovered the remains of a Viking settlement.

► Leif Eriksson points to the North American shore as he steers his ship through rough seas

FAKES AND FORGERIES

During the long search for Viking Vinland, a rune stone was found in Kensington, Minnesota, in 1898. It described an expedition in the area in 1362. A map showing the coast of North America, apparently mapped before Columbus's 1492 voyage, emerged in the 1950s. Both items are probably fakes, made by forgers eager to prove the truth of the sagas.

► The Kensington Rune Stone, which a local Swedish immigrant claimed to have found in 1898.

The end of the colonies

The Viking colonies in Vinland and Greenland did not last. Vinland first vanished after about 30 years, around CE 1030. Greenland disappeared around 1450. The Viking state in Iceland lost its independence to the kings of Norway in the mid-13th century, but the settlement there survived and became the modern state of Iceland.

THE END OF VINLAND

The Viking attempt to settle North America failed because there were not enough Viking Greenlanders to farm and build on the Vinland colony. They were also unable to defend themselves when the Native Americans attacked them. Vinland, though, had the resources the Vikings needed and voyages searching for these are recorded into the mid-1300s.

▼ *The Viking settlement in Newfoundland, Canada. The Vinland colony provided the Viking Greenlanders much-needed timber for building.*

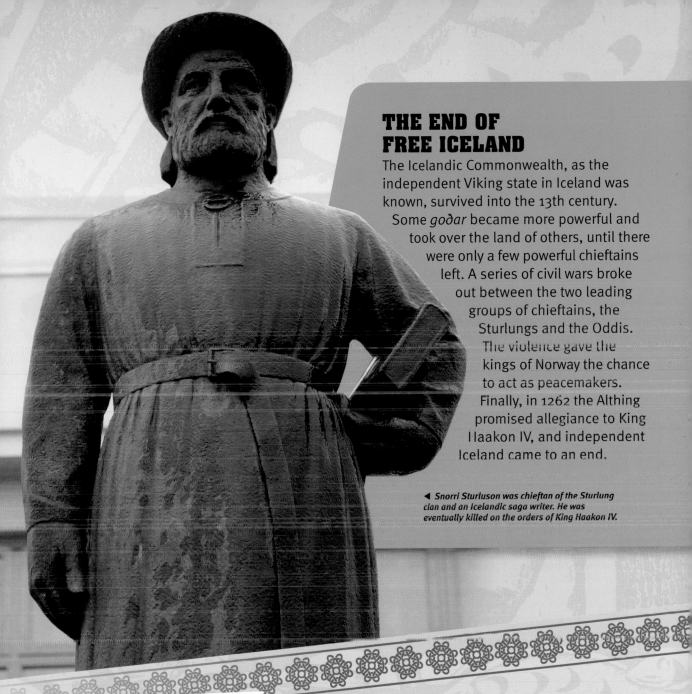

THE END OF FREE ICELAND

The Icelandic Commonwealth, as the independent Viking state in Iceland was known, survived into the 13th century. Some *goðar* became more powerful and took over the land of others, until there were only a few powerful chieftains left. A series of civil wars broke out between the two leading groups of chieftains, the Sturlungs and the Oddis. The violence gave the kings of Norway the chance to act as peacemakers. Finally, in 1262 the Althing promised allegiance to King Haakon IV, and independent Iceland came to an end.

◄ *Snorri Sturluson was chieftan of the Sturlung clan and an Icelandic saga writer. He was eventually killed on the orders of King Haakon IV.*

▲ *The ruins of a Viking church in Greenland, abandoned in the 15th century.*

THE MYSTERIOUS END OF VIKING GREENLAND

By the 1350s, Viking Greenland was facing difficulties. Voyages there became less frequent although remains dating to the early 1400s show there was some form of a community there. However, when a Danish expedition arrived in 1605, all traces of the Viking colony were gone. The reason for its disappearance is not clear. Cold weather, disease, or attacks by Inuit or pirates may be to blame.

Expansion to the east

Having settled on the southern shore of the Baltic Sea, Swedish Vikings pushed up the River Neva. They built a settlement at Staraya Ladoga near St. Petersburg in CE 750. They traded and, over time, they founded more settlements and a principality (a state ruled by a prince) at Kiev. This gave rise to medieval Russia and Ukraine.

▼ The fortress at Staraya Ladoga in Russia was built on the site of the original Viking fortress.

▲ Rurik was born around CE 830 and died in CE 879.

THE FOUNDATION OF VIKING RUS

In the east, the Vikings were known as **Rus**. The *Russian Primary Chronicle* tells that in CE 862, local Slavs invited three "Rus" brothers to rule over them. The eldest, Rurik, settled in Novgorod from where he controlled the others. His successor, Oleg, captured Kiev in CE 882 and made it the Rus capital. Archaeological evidence suggests that Rus settlements and trade were growing at this time.

ARAB ACCOUNTS OF THE VIKINGS

Some of the earliest accounts we have of the Viking Rus come from Arab traders or diplomats who travelled into the lands they controlled. The Persian geographer Ibn Rusteh wrote that the Rus had no villages, but that they wore clean garments and liked to wear gold arm rings. In contrast, the diplomat Ibn Fadlan said that the Rus were filthy and that they all shared the same bowl of water in which to wash.

Viking Russia

From their bases in Novgorod and Kiev, the Vikings controlled a large area of the great Russian rivers, such as the Volga. Over time, their rulers married into the local Slav families and became Christian. By the late 11th century CE, they had lost their Viking customs.

THE RURIK DYNASTY

Rurik's descendants established themselves in Kiev. In CE 907, Rurik's relative Oleg attacked Constantinople, the capital of the Byzantine empire. The Vikings attacked Constantinople again in CE 941 under Oleg's successor Igor, and in CE 943–944 they raided as far east as the Caspian Sea. Svyatoslav destroyed the mighty Khazar empire in CE 965. After this, the Rus gave up their Viking raiding ways and became more like a Slav kingdom.

▶ *In his attack on Constantinople, Oleg fixed his shield to the gates to show that he wanted to take the city.*

VLADIMIR OF KIEV

In CE 978, Prince Vladimir seized the throne in Kiev after a bitter civil war with his brothers. He needed support from powerful neighbors and planned to gain this by abandoning paganism in favour of either Islam, Judaism, or Christianity. In the end, he chose Constantinople's Orthodox Christianity, and married the sister of the Byzantine emperor, Basil II. However, links between Scandinavia and Kiev still remained strong.

◀ *Prince Vladimir is shown here being baptized an Orthodox Christian in CE 988.*

Th transform tion of the Viking world

From the 10th century CE, the Viking world began to change. In Denmark, Sweden, and Norway, strong rulers united the small chiefdoms into kingdoms. As royal power grew, governments got better at raising money through taxes and enforcing the law. Towns began to grow and Christianity took hold.

▲ *A gold ornament from the reign of Harald Bluetooth is stamped with a cross.*

UNIFIED KINGDOMS

Powerful dynasties emerged in Scandinavia in the 10th century CE and new kingdoms started to form. The process began first in Denmark under the Jelling Dynasty in the late 10th century CE, and continued until Sweden united in the 12th century. Gradually, the independent raiding that had been common in the early Viking Age died away.

▶ *This model shows the thriving trading town of Aarhus in Denmark as it may have looked in the 10th century CE. It was surrounded by a fortified wall for protection.*

Transformation	New kingdoms	Viking trade	Christianity
The Viking world begins to change from the 10th century CE onward (see pages 46–47).	In the 900s CE, small chiefdoms unify (unite) to create Viking kingdoms (see pages 48–51).	A vast trading network is established and riches are often buried for safe-keeping (see pages 52–53).	Christianity begins to take hold as kings convert to the religion from the 900s CE onwards (see pages 54–55).

GROWING TOWNS

There were very few towns in Scandinavia before the 9th century CE. Those that existed were trading centers, such as Aarhus in Denmark. From the early 11th century CE, new towns were established. Many, such as Sigtuna in Sweden and Oslo in Norway, were royal capitals or centers of government.

▲ Early Viking churches were stave churches, a style with a simple wooden structure, such as this one at Lomen, Norway.

CHRISTIANITY

Christian missionaries had traveled to Scandinavia in the 9th century CE. However, the faith did not take root until rulers such as Harald Bluetooth of Denmark and Olaf Tryggvason and Olaf Haraldsson of Norway converted to Christianity. As Christians, Viking rulers found themselves accepted and respected by other European kings. This change also contributed to the decline of raids from Scandinavia.

LAW CODES AND GOVERNMENT

As governments became stronger, they needed bigger bureaucracies to run them. Over time, important officials appointed by the kings gained influence similar to that of the European nobles. Law codes had governed Viking lands for centuries, but from the 11th century CE, royal legal decrees became more common.

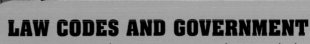

Growth of royal power
Olaf Haraldsson unifies Norway in CE 1020. Danish and Swedish royal power grows (see pages 56–58).

Government and law
Viking societies set up a system of local assemblies and kings issue law codes (see page 59).

Raids and battles
The Vikings return to England, attack Spain and the east, and are defeated in Ireland (see pages 60–65).

Viking Age ends
Harald Hardrada dies in CE 1066. Viking-style raids continue only on Scottish islands (see pages 66–69).

Unifying Denmark

▲ *Harald's baptism, shown on an altarpiece from Tamdrup, Denmark.*

Although there were kings in Denmark in the 9th and early 10th centuries CE, we know little about them. Around CE 930, Gorm the Old established a dynasty named after the royal center at Jelling. After Gorm's death, his son Harald Bluetooth unified the Danes under his rule and converted to Christianity.

HARALD BLUETOOTH

Harald had co-ruled with his father Gorm, but was still only 25 when he became king in CE 958. He strengthened royal rule by building fortresses, and fought wars against the Germans. These actions and his conversion to Christianity made the kingdom more unified, but they did not end the raiding. Harald's son Sweyn Forkbeard led a series of massive raids on England from CE 991, and became king there in CE 1013.

KEY

▮ Harald Bluetooth's kingdom

▮ Harald's vassal and ally states

0 ——— 200 miles

0 ——— 200 kilometers

SCANDINAVIA

VIK

DENMARK

▲ *Harald's kingdom is shown in orange, and his allies and vassal states (states dominated by him) are in blue.*

JELLING

Jelling was already a royal center under Gorm the Old. Harald Bluetooth built new monuments there, including a large burial mound, probably for his father's body. After he became a Christian, Harald built a second mound, founded a church, and set up a rune stone. On it he boasted that he had "won the whole of Denmark for himself" and "made the Danes Christian." The Jelling Stone was also carved with one of the first images of Christ's crucifixion to be made in Scandinavia.

◄ *Harald's rune stone with Christ on a cross, which stands in Jelling, Denmark.*

Th Tr ll borg fort– and the Danevirke

Harald Bluetooth strengthened Denmark's defenses in a number of ways. He needed to do this because of the threat from the Germans to the south, who sometimes attacked the Danish town of Hedeby. Harald also ordered the strengthening of existing defensive walls on the southern border, and improved Denmark's roads to allow his armies to travel faster.

THE TRELLEBORG FORTS

In the early 980s CE, Harald ordered the building of a series of large circular fortresses at strategic places in Denmark. They are known as Trelleborg forts and were named after the first one to be discovered at Trelleborg on Jutland. They range in size from Fyrkat (also on Jutland) and Nonnebakken (near Odense), which both measure 394 feet (120 m) across, to Aggersborg (in northern Jutland) which is 790 feet (241 m) across,

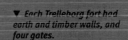
▼ Each Trelleborg fort had earth and timber walls, and four gates.

RAVNING ENGE AND THE DANEVIRKE

Harald also ordered the building of a 2, 460-foot (750-m) bridge across the marshy valley at Ravning Enge, south of Jelling. It involved the sinking of about 1200 wooden piles into the swamp. The effort needed to build this shows Harald's power in commanding the resources. He also supervised the strengthening of the **Danevirke**, a defensive wall around Hedeby at the southern end of Jutland.

◄ This is the Vejle Museum's reconstruction of the Ravning Bridge, which Harald built across the Vejle river valley around CE 980.

Harald's forts may only have been temporary, as he wood rotted and was not repaired.

49

Towns and trad

During the early Viking Age, there were only a handful of towns in Scandinavia. Most people lived on farms or in small villages. From the late 8th century CE, a few trading centers sprang up and these developed into small towns. A new wave of towns appeared 200 years later. These were known for crafts, trade, and as centers of royal power.

RIBE AND HEDEBY

Denmark's oldest town was Ribe in the southwest of Jutland. It emerged around CE 710 as a seasonal marketplace. About CE 780, permanent buildings were built and it became a thriving trading town, but was abandoned in the mid-9th century CE. Denmark's next town was Hedeby, which developed into an important Viking trading center from CE 800. It went into decline after it was sacked (destroyed) by Harald Hardrada of Norway in CE 1049. After that, most trading activity shifted to nearby Schleswig.

▲ *This coin found at Birka in Sweden was probably minted at Hedeby, Denmark.*

▲ *The inside of a reconstructed Viking building near the site of Hedeby.*

▲ Reconstructions of Viking boats at the settlement of Birka. The town was a vital link on the trade routes between Scandinavia and Russia.

KAUPANG

A small trading town emerged in southern Norway at Kaupang. It was founded in the early 9th century CE and probably disappeared a century later. Discoveries of glass and amber beads, textiles, brooches, belts, and jewelry show that it was a center for craft production. These craft items were sold on site or traded by merchants.

▲ Viking brooch

BIRKA

Built on a small island in Lake Mälaren, Birka was Sweden's first town. It flourished around CE 800 mainly as a trading settlement. Its merchants traveled as far as Staraya Ladoga in Russia and the Rhineland in Germany. It had some level of independence and even had its own assembly. By around CE 980, Birka no longer existed. Its trade may have been damaged by changes in the water levels of the lake and by the growth of the nearby town of Sigtuna.

▲ St Olof church in Sigtuna was built around 1100.

NEW TOWNS

Most of the early Scandinavian towns had disappeared by the late 10th century CE. Then a new wave of towns grew, many as royal capitals. In Sweden, Sigtuna grew under King Olof Skötkonung (CE 995–1022). In Norway, King Harald Hardrada established Oslo as his new capital in CE 1048 and Trondheim grew as a political center in the north. In Denmark, towns such as Aarhus and Roskilde began to replace Ribe and Hedeby.

Viking trade

Scandinavians were traders before they were raiders. Trade was very important to the Vikings. It was a way of importing the goods that the Vikings could not make themselves, often luxury items, and of exporting those goods that they had plenty of, such as furs.

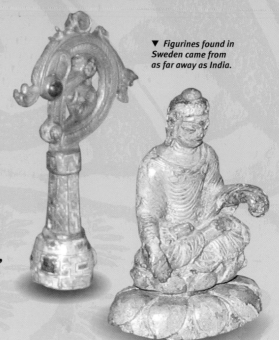

▼ Figurines found in Sweden came from as far away as India.

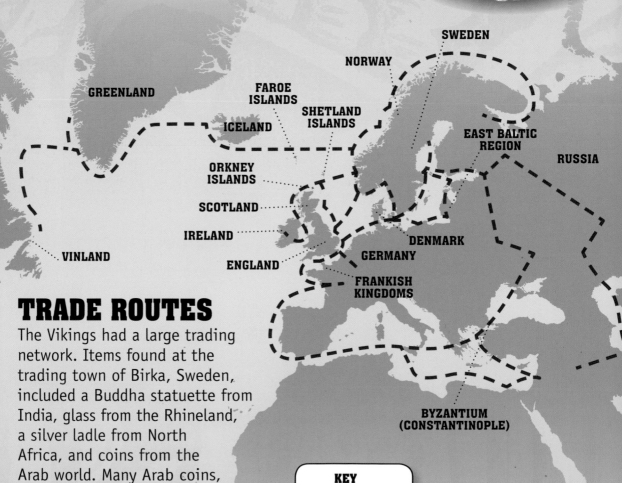

SWEDEN

NORWAY

GREENLAND

FAROE ISLANDS

SHETLAND ISLANDS

ICELAND

EAST BALTIC REGION

RUSSIA

ORKNEY ISLANDS

SCOTLAND

IRELAND

DENMARK

VINLAND

GERMANY

ENGLAND

FRANKISH KINGDOMS

BYZANTIUM (CONSTANTINOPLE)

TRADE ROUTES

The Vikings had a large trading network. Items found at the trading town of Birka, Sweden, included a Buddha statuette from India, glass from the Rhineland, a silver ladle from North Africa, and coins from the Arab world. Many Arab coins, called dirhams, arrived via trade with Vikings in Russia in the 9th and 10th centuries CE.

KEY

– – – Key trading routes

0   500 miles

0   500 kilometers

▲ Trading routes connected the farthest parts of the Viking world, such as Russia or Greenland, with the homelands in Scandinavia.

Viking hoards

▲ *Arab dirhams are mixed up with Anglo-Saxon silver pieces in this hoard find.*

Plunder from the Vikings' raids and the coins they received through trade were often buried for safekeeping. When the owners died these hoards were forgotten. The dates of the coins tell us a lot about when they were buried and where they came from.

THE CUERDALE HOARD

A huge hoard buried at Cuerdale, in Lancashire, UK, contained 7,500 coins and about 1,000 pieces of silver. It was probably buried around CE 905 by Vikings fleeing Ireland after they had been thrown out of Dublin by the Irish. It may have been payment for a mission to recapture Dublin. This did happen in CE 907, though clearly this treasure was not used to pay the warriors taking part. The hoard was found by workmen in 1840.

▲ *The Cuerdale hoard is the largest ever found in Western Europe. Each of the workmen who discovered it was allowed to keep a coin.*

GOTLAND

The small island of Gotland in the Baltic Sea off the east coast of Sweden is the site of the largest number of hoards in the Viking world. More than 700 hoards have been found there. A great deal of the wealth came from the Arab world, although it is not clear why there was so much. The Spillings hoard, the largest found on Gotland, contained 148 pounds (67 kg) of silver, including more than 14,000 coins (mainly Arab dirhams) and 486 silver arm rings, shown here.

▶ *The Spillings hoard was buried some time after CE 871, the date of the most recent coin found in the hoard.*

If you find a hoard with a metal detector, the value is shared with the owner of the land.

Conversion to Christianity

Some Vikings had become Christians after they lost battles to Christian rulers and agreed to be baptized. Christian missionaries, such as Anskar, also entered Scandinavia, but they didn't convert many people and their churches did not last long. Only when Viking kings began to convert in the 10th century CE did the new religion take hold.

▼ This image shows the Frankish missionary Anskar preaching to the Vikings at Birka, Sweden, in CE 829.

ICELAND AND SWEDEN

Several missionaries had tried to convert Iceland to Christianity, and they had won some followers. However, civil war threatened to break out between the pagan and Christian peoples. At the Althing assembly in CE 1000, both sides appealed to the Lawspeaker, Thorgeir Thorkelsson, to decide the matter. Although a pagan, Thorgeir ruled that all Icelanders must become Christian. Sweden remained pagan much longer than the other Viking regions—the great pagan cult center at Uppsala continued to worship the Norse gods until about CE 1090.

◄ This Viking Age crucifix was found in Lund, Sweden.

Even after converting, many Icelanders continued the pagan practice of eating horsemeat.

THE CONVERSION OF DENMARK

In CE 950, Harald Bluetooth welcomed the Christian **missionary** Poppo to his court. At a feast, Harald argued that Christ was less powerful than the Viking gods Odin and Thor. When Poppo disagreed, Harald challenged him to prove Christ's power. Poor Poppo had to hold a lump of red-hot iron and then have his hand wrapped in bandages. If the wound did not become infected, he would win his case. Several days later, Poppo's bandages were unwrapped and his wound was clean. Harald was won over and converted to Christianity, and many of his nobles followed.

◀ This church at Jelling, Denmark, stands on the site of the church built by Harald Bluetooth in CE 965.

▶ A statue of Olaf Haraldsson from Leikanger Church in Norway. He became Norway's patron saint.

OLAF TRYGGVASON AND OLAF HARALDSSON

Attempts to convert Norway to Christianity began under Håkon the Good in CE 936, but this upset many nobles and Håkon went back to paganism. His great nephew Olaf Tryggvason, who became king in CE 995, destroyed the pagan centers. However, he had made little progress by the time of his death in battle in CE 1000. Norway finally became Christian under Olaf Haraldsson, who defeated his rivals for the throne in CE 1016. He had pagan women burnt as witches and banned pagan festivals. His brutality led to a revolt and his death at the Battle of Stiklestad in CE 1030 (see page 57), but his son Magnus continued to spread Christianity, and he became a saint.

The growth of royal power in Norway

Norway had been partly unified by Harald Finehair, who ruled from CE 872–930. He expanded the area around Oslo to control much of the west of the country. But after his death, Norway was dominated by the kings of Denmark for most of the 10th century CE. It was only when Olaf Tryggvason became king in CE 995 that the country started to unite.

▲ Olaf Tryggvason used force to convert the Norwegians to Christianity, with mixed results.

OLAF TRYGGVASON

Olaf was the son of a minor king in eastern Norway. He began his career as a raider, and joined a major attack against London in CE 994. After that, he returned to Norway to defeat his rivals, the **Jarls** of Hladir. He was accepted as king at an assembly at Gula in CE 996. Olaf became involved in a war with Denmark, and died during a naval battle.

▼ A smaller Danish fleet captured King Olaf's larger flagship (the middle boat) at the Battle of Svolder in CE 1000. Olaf is said to have leapt into the water and was never seen again.

OLAF HARALDSSON

After Olaf Tryggvason's death, Norway was divided between Sweden and the Jarls of Hladir. Then, in CE 1014 Olaf Haraldsson, whose father had ruled a region in southeast Norway, gave up a career as a raider to return home. He defeated the Jarls of Hladir in CE 1016 and claimed all of Norway for himself, ruling as King Olaf II. However, opposition to him grew, and in CE 1028 he was forced to flee. In CE 1030, he returned with an army of Russian and Swedish Vikings, but was killed at the Battle of Stiklestad.

11TH-CENTURY NORWAY

A brief period of Danish rule followed Olaf Haraldsson's death, but Olaf's son Magnus reclaimed the throne in CE 1035. Magnus made sure that Norway remained united. He even briefly managed to occupy Denmark in CE 1045. Magnus's uncle and successor, Harald Hardrada, died in battle in England in CE 1066 (see page 67). However, royal power was now so firmly established in Norway that the kingdom did not fall apart.

Royalty in Denmark and Sweden

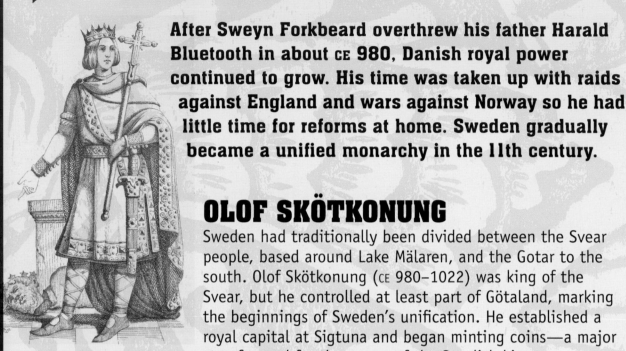

After Sweyn Forkbeard overthrew his father Harald Bluetooth in about CE 980, Danish royal power continued to grow. His time was taken up with raids against England and wars against Norway so he had little time for reforms at home. Sweden gradually became a unified monarchy in the 11th century.

▲ King Olof Skötkonung was baptized a Christian.

OLOF SKÖTKONUNG

Sweden had traditionally been divided between the Svear people, based around Lake Mälaren, and the Gotar to the south. Olof Skötkonung (CE 980–1022) was king of the Svear, but he controlled at least part of Götaland, marking the beginnings of Sweden's unification. He established a royal capital at Sigtuna and began minting coins—a major step forward for the power of the Swedish kings.

MEDIEVAL SWEDEN

Under Olof's sons, Anund Jakob and Emund the Old, a series of civil wars broke out until it looked like Sweden might fall apart. Strong royal rule under Sverker I (1130–1156) was followed by further civil wars. It was not until the mid-13th century that Sweden became a strong monarchy once more, with taxation and a national law code. These developments had occurred in Denmark and Norway long before.

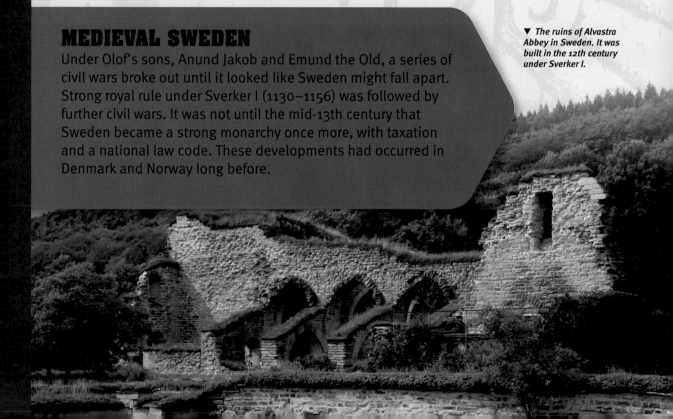

▼ The ruins of Alvastra Abbey in Sweden. It was built in the 12th century under Sverker I.

Viking law and government

Although Viking societies had chieftains, nobles, and kings with greater authority, they also had a system of local assemblies, known as "things." The things made decisions on legal matters and sometimes made laws. The kings also issued law codes to cover the lands under their rule.

THINGS AND ASSEMBLIES

Things came from the ancient tradition that free men could take part in decisions equally. In CE 996, Olaf Tryggvason declared himself king of Norway at the Gula Thing, which showed that even local assemblies were important bodies. The most famous thing was Iceland's Althing, which judged legal cases for the whole country.

▼ *Things were held at the prehistoric mounds at Anundshog in Sweden.*

▲ *The Grey Goose Laws may have got their name because they were written using a goose feather quill.*

LAW CODES

There was a body of traditional law in Scandinavian society, but over time kings started to issue law codes. Iceland had its own laws, issued by the Althing, which were known as the *Grágás* ("Grey Goose Laws"). When the Norwegians took control of Iceland, they issued a new law code, the *Járnsíða* ("Iron Side Laws"). These laws covered a wide range of matters, from regulating trade to laying down punishments for robbery and murder.

Cnut and th North Sea empire

Nearly 30 years after the fall of York, the Vikings returned in force to England in the 980s CE, during the reign of Aethelred the Unready. Thirty years of raids and invasions followed, until England fell once more to the Vikings, under Sweyn Forkbeard and his son Cnut.

▲ *Harold I, 'Harold Harefoot' (CE 1016–1040), as featured on this silver penny, was the son of Cnut.*

▶ *A statue honouring Byrhtnoth, who was killed at the Battle of Maldon.*

THE BATTLE OF MALDON

In CE 991, a huge Viking army, led by Olaf Tryggvason, the future king of Norway, landed in Essex. They were trapped on Northey Island near Maldon, but Byrhtnoth, the local Anglo-Saxon ealdorman (a senior local official), let them over the causeway to the mainland to ensure a fair fight. The Vikings rushed over and defeated the Anglo-Saxon army, killing Byrhtnoth and many other nobles. For the next 20 years, England suffered regular Viking raids.

▼ *The site of the Battle of Maldon near Northey Island on the Essex coast.*

Aethelred was only around 10 years old when he first became king of England.

62

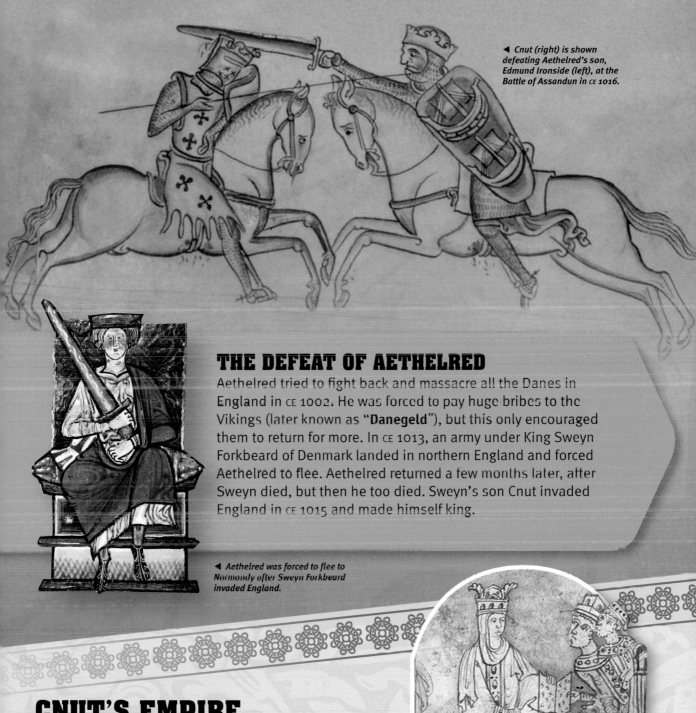

◀ Cnut (right) is shown defeating Aethelred's son, Edmund Ironside (left), at the Battle of Assandun in CE 1016.

THE DEFEAT OF AETHELRED

Aethelred tried to fight back and massacre all the Danes in England in CE 1002. He was forced to pay huge bribes to the Vikings (later known as "**Danegeld**"), but this only encouraged them to return for more. In CE 1013, an army under King Sweyn Forkbeard of Denmark landed in northern England and forced Aethelred to flee. Aethelred returned a few months later, after Sweyn died, but then he too died. Sweyn's son Cnut invaded England in CE 1015 and made himself king.

◀ Aethelred was forced to flee to Normandy after Sweyn Forkbeard invaded England.

CNUT'S EMPIRE

Cnut (also known as Canute) had many Scandinavian followers with him. He rewarded them with land and titles. In CE 1019, he returned to Denmark where he became king after his brother Harald died. In the 1020s CE, he also occupied part of Norway, creating an empire that stretched right across the North Sea. Cnut died in CE 1035, but Danish Viking rule over England lasted until CE 1042, when the Anglo-Saxon prince Edward the Confessor became king.

▲ Aethelred's widow, Queen Emma with her sons. Cnut married Emma in CE 1017.

61

The Norman conquest of England

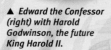
Edward the Confessor (right) with Harold Godwinson, the future King Harold II.

By CE 1042, an Anglo-Saxon was once again on the English throne. Aethelred's son, Edward the Confessor, had strong links to Normandy, where he had lived as a boy. When he died childless in CE 1066, the crown passed to Harold Godwinson, but the Norman Duke William claimed that Edward had left the English crown to him. William invaded, defeated Godwinson, and became king. Once again, England had a ruler of Viking origin.

▼ *A scene from the Bayeux Tapestry showing the knights of the Norman army charging into battle on horseback.*

WILLIAM THE CONQUEROR

William was connected to the English royal house by marriage—his great-grandfather was the brother of Aethelred's wife, Emma. He claimed that Edward the Confessor had promised him the throne and also that Harold Godwinson had sworn to help him become king during a visit to Normandy in CE 1065. When William heard that Edward the Confessor had died in January CE 1066, he assembled an army and a fleet and landed in England at Pevensey, in Sussex.

The appearance of a comet early in CE 1066 was seen as a bad omen for England.

64

HAROLD'S CAMPAIGNS

Harold Godwinson had to fight against two invasions. First, there was an invasion by Harald Hardrada of Norway, who believed he should be the next English king (see page 67). Godwinson marched rapidly north to meet them. At Stamford Bridge in Yorkshire he defeated the Norwegians in battle and killed Harald Hardrada. He then had to rush south to meet the Normans. As a result, Godwinson's troops were exhausted when they reached Hastings, near where William's army was camped on October 13 CE 1066.

▲ William was crowned king of England on Christmas Day CE 1066 at Westminster Abbey.

NORMAN RULE

William marched through Kent and on to London, where the royal councillors accepted him as king. A Viking descendant was now king of England. There were several further threats of attacks from Scandinavian kings and a small-scale attack in CE 1069 by Sweyn Estrithsson of Denmark, but after this, there were no more Viking raids on England.

THE BATTLE OF HASTINGS

On the morning of the battle, the Anglo-Saxon army assembled on a ridge and formed a shield wall. The Normans charged several times but could not break through the enemy lines. The shield wall weakened when some Anglo-Saxons broke rank, chased the Normans and were killed. The Anglo-Saxon army collapsed after Harold Godwinson was killed later in the afternoon. Tradition says that he was killed by an arrow that struck him in the eye.

▶ Harold is struck by an arrow through the eye during the Battle of Hastings.

The end of Viking Ireland

The Vikings had retaken Dublin in CE 907, but by the late 10th century CE they were being attacked by neighbouring Irish kingdoms. When Irish king Brian Bóruma defeated an army that included Vikings, Viking power in Ireland started to decline. The remaining Viking outposts became part of the Irish kingdoms.

FROM OLAF CUARÁN TO SIHTRIC SILKENBEARD

Olaf Cuarán, once a Viking king of York, returned to Ireland to rule Dublin from CE 951 to 980. His reign ended in a terrible defeat to Máel Sechnaill of Meath at the Battle of Tara. After this, the Vikings had to make alliances with Irish rulers to survive. Dublin's Viking ruler Sihtric Silkenbeard was forced to submit to Brian Bóruma.

▲ Irish king Brian Bóruma (right) faces an armed Viking at the Battle of Clontarf.

▼ The Battle of Clontarf, which lasted from sunrise to sunset on April 23, CE 1014, ended in heavy loss of life on both sides.

THE BATTLE OF CLONTARF

Sihtric Silkenbeard decided to fight back and gathered together a force made up of Viking and Irish allies. At the Battle of Clontarf in CE 1014, they were heavily defeated, although Brian Bóruma himself was killed. Sihtric remained king of Dublin, but Viking power was broken. There were still Norse speakers in Dublin in the 1170s, when the English invaded, but they no longer had any political influence.

Vikings in the south

The Vikings raided far into southern Europe, attacking Spain in CE 844. They also raided as far east as the Caspian Sea in CE 912 and CE 1040. In addition, they attacked the great capital of the Byzantine empire, Constantinople, which is now the city of Istanbul in Turkey.

▲ *The Ingvar rune stone was made in memory of Viking warriors who died in the expedition to the Caspian Sea.*

THE VARANGIAN GUARD

Vikings from Kiev attacked Constantinople—which they called Miklagard ("the great city")—four times between CE 860 and CE 944. But after his marriage to a Byzantine princess in CE 988, Vladimir of Kiev (see page 45) sent 6000 warriors to Constantinople to serve in the imperial bodyguard. These Vikings, known as "Varangians," served the emperor for more than 200 years, and fought in military campaigns as far away as Sicily and Syria.

HASTEINN AND BJORN

The most famous southern Viking raid was that of Hasteinn and Bjorn Ironside in CE 859. They attacked Muslim-controlled Cádiz in Spain, landed in Morocco, and burned towns in southern France. They even tried to capture Rome, but settled for Luni, a smaller Italian city. A saga tells how the pair tricked the citizens of Luni into letting them hold a Viking funeral inside the city gates, before the two of them sprung out of the coffin and attacked the city.

◀ *Varangians (Viking guards) hand possessions to a woman.*

Harald Hardrada

As the Viking Age came to an end, there were still men who fought and raided in the old Viking style. Harald Hardrada, half-brother of King Olaf Haraldsson (see page 57), started fighting in CE 1030 as a 15-year-old at the Battle of Stiklestad, where Olaf was killed. He then spent years in exile in Russia, joined the Varangian Guard, and became king of Norway. He died fighting during his invasion of England in CE 1066.

▶ Harald's half-brother, King Olaf Haraldsson, is shown here being killed at the Battle of Stiklestad.

HARALD IN RUSSIA

After the Battle of Stiklestad in CE 1030, a wounded Harald Hardrada hid with friendly farmers until he could take a ship to Russia. There, Grand Prince Yaroslav of Kiev made him a commander in his army. He fought in several wars in the Baltic and against neighboring Slavic tribes. When he fell in love with Yaroslavl's daughter Ellisif, the Grand Prince insisted that Harald seek further military glory before being allowed to marry her.

Harald received the nickname "Hardrada" ("hard ruler") when he was king of Norway.

68

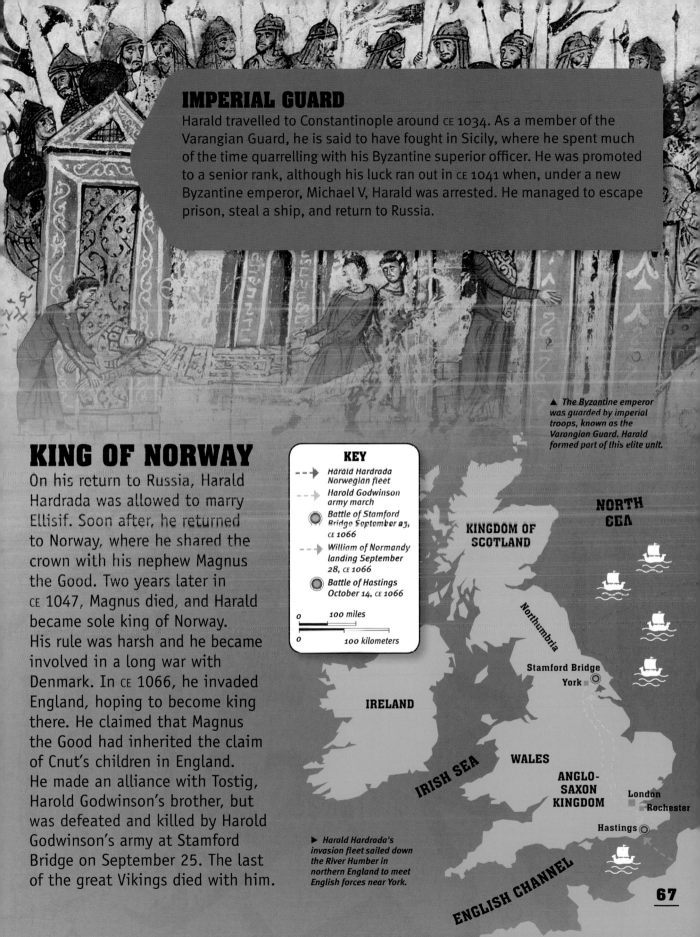

IMPERIAL GUARD

Harald travelled to Constantinople around CE 1034. As a member of the Varangian Guard, he is said to have fought in Sicily, where he spent much of the time quarrelling with his Byzantine superior officer. He was promoted to a senior rank, although his luck ran out in CE 1041 when, under a new Byzantine emperor, Michael V, Harald was arrested. He managed to escape prison, steal a ship, and return to Russia.

▲ The Byzantine emperor was guarded by imperial troops, known as the Varangian Guard. Harald formed part of this elite unit.

KING OF NORWAY

On his return to Russia, Harald Hardrada was allowed to marry Ellisif. Soon after, he returned to Norway, where he shared the crown with his nephew Magnus the Good. Two years later in CE 1047, Magnus died, and Harald became sole king of Norway. His rule was harsh and he became involved in a long war with Denmark. In CE 1066, he invaded England, hoping to become king there. He claimed that Magnus the Good had inherited the claim of Cnut's children in England. He made an alliance with Tostig, Harold Godwinson's brother, but was defeated and killed by Harold Godwinson's army at Stamford Bridge on September 25. The last of the great Vikings died with him.

KEY

- - -▶ Harald Hardrada Norwegian fleet
- - -▶ Harold Godwinson army march
◉ Battle of Stamford Bridge September 25, CE 1066
- - -▶ William of Normandy landing September 28, CE 1066
◉ Battle of Hastings October 14, CE 1066

0 — 100 miles
0 — 100 kilometers

KINGDOM OF SCOTLAND

NORTH SEA

Northumbria

Stamford Bridge
York ◉

IRELAND

IRISH SEA

WALES

ANGLO-SAXON KINGDOM

London
Rochester

Hastings ◉

▶ Harald Hardrada's invasion fleet sailed down the River Humber in northern England to meet English forces near York.

ENGLISH CHANNEL

Twilight of the Viking world

By the 11th century ce, the great age of the Viking raids was over. Scandinavian kings were more powerful and they no longer encouraged the kind of attacks that were once common. Only a few places, such as the Scottish islands, continued with the old way of life. Its warriors continued raiding for another 100 years.

MAGNUS BARELEGS

The kings of Norway had long wanted to rule over the Viking settlements in the Scottish islands. In CE 1098, an expedition was launched by Harald Hardrada's grandson Magnus Barelegs (he got his nickname because he liked to wear a kilt). Magnus made his son Sigurd ruler of the islands. He then sailed to the Irish Sea and attacked the Isle of Man and Anglesey. He returned in 1102, but was killed in an attack on the north of Ireland.

◄ *This modern statue in Sweden shows Erik Evergood of Denmark, Inge the Elder of Sweden, and Magnus Barelegs of Norway.*

Magnus Barelegs was the last Norwegian king to die in battle abroad.

THE LAST RAIDS

The last recorded old-style Viking raider was Svein Asleifsson of Gairsay in the Orkney Islands. Twice a year, he and his 80 warriors would take ships and steal goods from around the Hebrides and Ireland. In 1171, Earl Harald of Orkney tried to persuade the old warrior to hang up his ax, but Svein only promised to do so after carrying out one last raid. He attacked Dublin, but his force fell into hidden traps the Dubliners had dug outside the city and all the Vikings were killed.

▼ *The ruins of Bucholie Castle in Caithness, Scotland. A fortress called Lamaborg was first built on the site by Viking raider Svein Asleifsson in 1140.*

HÅKON THE OLD

King Håkon the Old of Norway (1204–1263) had forced the Viking settlements in Iceland and Greenland to accept him as king. He then tried to do the same to the Viking colonies in the Hebrides. He set out in 1263 for Scotland but his army was trapped by a storm and defeated by the Scots. Håkon returned to Orkney where he fell ill and died. On his deathbed, he had the old saga stories read out to him—the last of the Vikings listening to the heroic deeds of his ancestors.

▲ *The Bergenhaus fortress in Bergen, Norway, was built during the reign of Håkon the Old.*

The Viking legacy

The legacy of the Vikings lives on centuries after their raids ended. Along with the memory of their actions in sagas and histories, Viking influence can still be seen in the words of many languages, especially English. More recently, writers and film-makers have turned to the Vikings as a source for novels, television programs and movies.

Other English words of Viking origin include "ugly," "gap," "cake," and "jolly."

THE VIKING LANGUAGE

The Viking colonies in the Faroes and Iceland kept their languages and a type of Old Norse is still spoken there today. In the Scottish islands, a language called Norn was spoken and survived into the early 19th century in Orkney. Elsewhere, many words of Norse origin survive in English, such as "egg," "bread," "sky," "dirt," "law," and even "they." This shows that Danish and English speakers interacted with one another for a long time in the Danelaw. In Irish, words concerning ships and commerce were borrowed, such as "ancaire" (anchor), "stiúir" (rudder), and "margadh" (market).

Viking language
Viking words still remain in many dialects and languages, particularly in English (see page 70).

Viking heritage
The 19th century sees a growing interest in the Viking heritage in Scandinavia (see page 71).

Nordic warriors
In the 1930s and 1940s, the German Nazis portray Vikings as the ultimate warriors (see page 71).

Viking traditions
Interest in the Viking past sees a resurgence of Viking traditions, such as Up-Helly-Aa (see page 72).

REDISCOVERY OF THE VIKINGS

In the 19th century, there was a renewed interest in Scandinavia about the Viking past. People studied their poems and published journals about Viking history. In Norway, a growing movement pushing for independence from Denmark led to more interest in the country's early history. This resulted in the sailing of a replica Viking ship from Norway to America in 1893. This interest in the past also had a darker side, and in the 1930s and 1940s Germany's Nazi party tried to promote interest in its racist ideas by portraying the Vikings as the ultimate warriors.

◀ *This replica Viking ship was built in Norway and sailed to the United States in 1893.*

▲ *A poster from the 1940s tries to recruit Norwegians to the German forces. The Nazis considered the Nordic people, who were descended from the Vikings, a superior race.*

Books and comics
Writers use the Viking era as the setting for their stories in books and comics (see page 73).

Film and television
The Vikings become a popular theme for films and television programs (see page 73).

Viking archaeology
Viking remains are conserved or rebuilt to provide an insight into the Viking past (see page 74).

Viking ancestry
Traces of Viking DNA can be found in former Viking colonies, including Iceland and Britain (see page 75).

Reinvention of the Vikings

Enthusiasm for Viking history revived in the 19th century. This was because people were becoming more interested in Europe's past, especially in Scandinavia. Art and music portrayed the Vikings as heroic and romantic figures.

UP-HELLY-AA

Popular interest in the Vikings has led to the revival of traditions thought to be from the Viking past. In Lerwick in the Shetland Islands, on the last Tuesday in January, the festival of Up-Helly-Aa is celebrated. Shetlanders dressed as Viking warriors parade through the streets of Lerwick. They then set light to a model of a Viking longship.

VIKING COSTUME

In 1811, an association was founded in Stockholm to promote the study of Viking history. Viking balls were held, where people dressed in costume and horned helmets, which they thought was the Viking style (in fact, the Vikings never wore such helmets). Interest in the Vikings was very strong in Norway, which at that time was ruled by Denmark. Norwegians were eager to celebrate the glorious past of Olaf Tryggvason and Harald Hardrada.

▲ Once the ship has burned and the flames died down, a night of partying begins.

Vikings in popular culture

During the Viking Age, the exploits of the Vikings were already popular themes for stories. Sagas told of the adventures of Viking warriors and kings. In the 1800s, writers used the Viking Age as a setting for their stories. In the 20th century, Viking-themed books, comics, and films were popular.

▶ Wagner merged tales from Norse and German mythology when writing The Ring of the Nibelung.

OPERA

The German composer Richard Wagner used Viking sagas as source material for his epic opera cycle *The Ring of the Nibelung*. The four parts that make up the cycle were first performed from 1869–1876.

▲ The One Ring from the film version of J R R Tolkien's The Lord of the Rings. *The plot was influenced by Viking mythology and other folk and fairy tales.*

LITERATURE AND FILM

Viking stories have inspired modern literature, television, and films. Children's stories such as *Noggin the Nog* (which features a "King of the Northmen") and J R R Tolkien's *The Lord of the Rings* were influenced by Norse myths. Alan Garner's *The Weirdstone of Brisingamen* mentions the legend of Ragnarök. In 1958, a major Hollywood movie called *The Vikings* was made, while the 2010 computer-animated film *How to Train Your Dragon* takes place in a mythical Viking world.

The four parts of *The Ring of the Nibelung* take more than 15 hours to perform.

Viking archaeology

Many Viking sites have been destroyed or lost over time. However, a few places have been conserved in good condition, or have been rebuilt. These give a good idea of what Viking places looked like a thousand years ago.

◄ A cross found at a Viking site in Dumfries, Scotland.

ICELAND AND GREENLAND

In Iceland, a Viking farm at Stöng, which was once buried in volcanic ash, can now be seen. The remains of Iceland's oldest longhouse have also been uncovered in Reykjavik. It may date from the late 9th century CE. Many of the sites of Greenland's original Western Settlement can be visited, including Brattahlid, the farm of Erik the Red.

DENMARK

The rune stones at Jelling on Jutland can be visited today. They were set up by Gorm the Old and Harald Bluetooth. Inside the museum, the rune stones are painted in their original vivid colors. At Trelleborg in Jutland the circular fort built by Harald Bluetooth has been reconstructed. The gates and the huge earth ramparts which once defended the site can be made out.

▼ Reproduction of a Viking longhouse at L'Anse aux Meadows, Newfoundland, Canada.

L'ANSE AUX MEADOWS, CANADA

The remains of a small Viking settlement have been conserved at L'Anse aux Meadows on Newfoundland, Canada, next to a reconstructed Viking village. The settlement was excavated in the 1960s, proving that the Vikings had visited North America.

The spread of the Vikings

Many Vikings settled in their overseas colonies, such as England, Ireland, and Scotland. Traces of their DNA (genetic information) can be found in their present-day offspring. In Iceland, the population is almost entirely of Scandinavian origin. In Greenland and North America, however, the Viking colonies disappeared. As a result, there is no trace of the Vikings in the DNA of the people living there today.

▼ This Icelandic mother and son are typically Scandinavian in appearance.

DNA STUDIES

A major study in Britain in 2014 found that 25 percent of the people of Orkney, Scotland, had Norwegian ancestors. Elsewhere, the study did not find direct evidence of Scandinavian migration to England. However, it is sometimes difficult to tell the difference between DNA from Scandinavia and DNA from the homelands of the Anglo-Saxons who invaded England in the 5th and 6th centuries CE.

VIKING WOMEN COLONISTS

A DNA study in 2014 showed that Viking women had accompanied their men to the colonies in Orkney, Shetland, and Iceland. The DNA of modern Icelanders also shows that about half of the women in the original population of Iceland were of Celtic origin. This suggests that the Vikings must also have brought Scottish and Irish women along with them.

Until DNA testing, many on Orkney had thought their ancestry was Irish, not Viking.

WHO'S WHO?
The Viking world

The Viking rulers were famed as powerful warriors, and their deeds were told in the many Viking sagas. They sailed great distances from their Scandinavian homeland, and raided and conquered lands across Europe and beyond. They also left behind beautiful works of art. Here are some of the notable Viking figures.

Ragnar Lodbrok
(d. 800s CE)

A legendary Viking leader, who was said to have invaded England and been put to death by Aelle, king of Northumbria.

Ivar the Boneless
(d. CE 869)

With his brothers, Haldfan and Ubba, Ivar led the Great Army which invaded England in CE 865 and most of the Anglo-Saxon kingdoms.

Rurik
(CE 830–CE 879)

The Slavs invited him to rule in Russia. He became the ruler of Novgorod and his descendants are the ancestors of medieval Russia.

Guthrum
(d. CE 890)

A Danish king who conquered Mercia in CE 873–874. He invaded Wessex in early CE 878 and settled in East Anglia until his death.

Ingólfur Arnarson
(d. c. CE 903)

With his brother-in-law Hjorleifur, Arnarson divided up the uninhabited island of Iceland and founded a Viking colony there around CE 874.

Rollo (or Hrolf)
(d. CE 928)

Leader who made a treaty in CE 911 with Charles the Simple of France. The land Rollo gained formed the core of the Duchy of Normandy.

Harald Bluetooth
(d. CE 988)

The first Christian ruler of Denmark. He extended his authority from Jutland to cover all of Denmark, unifying the kingdom.

Olaf Tryggvason
(c. CE 968–CE 1000)

Olaf was a raider in the Baltic and in England. In CE 995, he became king of Norway and tried to promote Christianity there.

Erik the Red
(d. CE 1002)

Erik was the first Viking to land and settle on Greenland. His son Leif is said to have discovered Vinland in North America.

Sweyn Forkbeard
(CE 960–CE 1014)

King of Denmark, England and parts of Norway, Forkbeard was the son of Harald Bluetooth and the father of Cnut the Great.

Olaf Haraldsson
(CE 995–CE 1030)

Norway became fully Christian when Haraldsson became King Olaf II in CE 1016. He faced opposition to his rule and was killed in battle.

Cnut the Great
(d. CE 1035)

Son of Sweyn Forkbeard, Cnut became king of England in CE 1016 and Denmark in CE 1018. He also ruled much of Sweden and part of Norway.

Harald Hardrada
(CE 1015–CE 1066)

Harald Hardrada lived in Sweden, Russia and Constantinople. He shared the kingship of Norway with his nephew and died in England in 1066.

Magnus Barelegs
(CE 1073–1103)

Grandson of Harald Hardrada, Magnus Barelegs was the king of Norway. He established control of the Orkney Islands and was killed in Ireland.

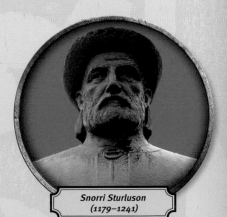

Snorri Sturluson
(1179–1241)

Icelandic politician, saga writer and historian. He was killed on the orders of King Haakon IV of Norway.

GLOSSARY

AESIR
One of the two main groups of Viking gods. This was the principal group and included Odin, Thor, and Frigg.

ANGLO-SAXON
A tribe of people who were living in Britain during the Viking Age. They were descended from Germanic tribes who migrated from mainland Europe.

ASGARD
One of the realms of the Viking world, and the place where the gods lived.

BAPTIZED
To be formally welcomed into the Christian church. The ceremony usually involves water being poured over the head.

BERSERKER
A Viking warrior who fought in a trance-like fury.

DANEGELD
A sum of money paid to Viking raiders to stop them from attacking a region.

DANELAW
The name given to a part of England settled and controlled by the Vikings. It was created by a treaty between Alfred the Great and the Vikings around CE 880.

DANEVIRKE
A system of defensive walls built by the Vikings to stop German invaders.

ELVIDNER
The hall of misery and cold where Hel ruled over the dead.

GODAR
A Nordic word for chieftain. Goðar representatives sat in the Althing national assembly in Iceland.

JARL
The name given to a member of a Viking royal family.

LONGHOUSE
A typical Viking house, which was long and thin. It contained very little furniture and may have also housed farm animals.

LONGPHORT
The name given to a Viking naval base built in Ireland where Vikings could set out and raid nearby areas.

MIDGARD
Also known as "Middle Earth," Midgard was the Viking realm where humans lived.

MISSIONARY
Someone from a religious group who travels to another region to try to persuade the people living there to follow their own religion.

NORSE
The name given to something or someone who came from Scandinavia during the Viking Age.

PAGAN
Someone or something that is not related to one of the world's main religions. Many pagan religions have a number of different gods who control different parts of people's lives.

RUNES
The name given to the letters used by the Vikings. The letters were formed from straight lines which made them easy to carve into wood or stone.

RUNE STONE
A tall stone that was covered in runes and erected by the Vikings to celebrate a particular person or event.

RUS
The name given to the Vikings living to the east of the Baltic Sea. Their society formed the basis of what became Russia and Ukraine.

SHIELD WALL
A military formation where soldiers form a line of overlapping shields which is very difficult for enemy troops to break through.

SKRAELING
The name given by Viking settlers to the Native Americans they met in North America. The term means "wretches."

THING
The name given to a local assembly in Viking society. Things met to create laws, decide arguments, and judge criminals.

UTGARD
Meaning "the outer place," this was one of the realms of the Viking world, and the place where evil beings lived.

VALHALLA
The great hall of the god Odin, where he feasted with the souls of Vikings who had died bravely in battle.

VALKYRIES
The female spirits who carried the souls of brave Vikings from the battlefield to Odin's hall, Valhalla.

VANIR
One of the two main groups of Viking gods. This group was made up of the lesser gods.

VARANGIANS
Vikings who travelled to Russia. An elite group of Varangians guarded the Byzantine emperor in Constantinople.

YGGDRASIL
The mythical ash tree whose roots held the realms of the Viking world together.

INDEX